To Give and To Receive

American Alliance of Museums

The American Alliance of Museums has been bringing museums together since 1906, helping to develop standards and best practices, gathering and sharing knowledge, and providing advocacy on issues of concern to the entire museum community. Representing more than 35,000 individual museum professionals and volunteers, institutions, and corporate partners serving the museum field, the Alliance stands for the broad scope of the museum community.

The American Alliance of Museums' mission is to champion museums and nurture excellence in partnership with its members and allies.

Books published by AAM further the Alliance's mission to make standards and best practices for the broad museum community widely available.

To Give and To Receive

A Handbook on Collection Gifts and Donations for Museums and Donors

Second Edition

Edited by
SHARON SMITH THEOBALD

ROWMAN & LITTLEFIELD

Lanham • Boulder • New York • London

Published by Rowman & Littlefield
A wholly owned subsidiary of The Rowman & Littlefield Publishing Group, Inc.
4501 Forbes Boulevard, Suite 200, Lanham, Maryland 20706
www.rowman.com

6 Tinworth Street, London SE11 5AL, United Kingdom

British Library Cataloguing in Publication Information Available

Library of Congress Cataloging-in-Publication Data

Library of Congress Control Number: 2020934259
ISBN: 978-1-5381-2883-1 (cloth : alk. paper)
ISBN: 978-1-5381-2884-8 (pbk. : alk. paper)
ISBN: 978-1-5381-2885-5 (electronic)

♾™ The paper used in this publication meets the minimum requirements of American National Standard for Information Sciences—Permanence of Paper for Printed Library Materials, ANSI/NISO Z39.48-1992.

Contents

PART THREE
The IRS Perspective
compiled and edited by Laurette E. McCarthy

PART FOUR
Gift Considerations and Perspectives

PART FIVE

Ownership Perspectives and Fair Market Value

PART SIX

Tax Perspectives for Museums:
Review of Changes to the Pension Protection Act
(IRS Notice 2006-96)

Acknowledgments

I WISH TO THANK Beth J. Parker Miller, Amy McKune, and Romy Vreeland without whom this 2020 edition would not be possible. Appreciation is extended to Danielle Johnson, PhD, for her thoughtful insights and recommendations for the entire manuscript, as well as Jayne Hustead and Charlotte Harrington, who edited the case notes. The content of this publication was developed with the cooperation and involvement of an advisory committee consisting of museum professionals, dealers, collectors, and attorneys familiar with both museums and current tax laws.

I also thank the Advisory Committee members:

Helen A. Harrison, the Eugene V. and Clare E. Thaw Director of the Pollock-Krasner House and Study Center, the former home and studio of Jackson Pollock and Lee Krasner, a National Historic Landmark, in East Hampton, New York.

Scott Hodes, senior counsel, Bryan Cave Leighton Paisner LLP, Chicago. Life member, National Museum of Mexican Art, Chicago. Counsel to the Chicago Bauhaus Foundation.

MacKenzie Mallon, specialist, Provenance, Nelson-Atkins Museum of Art.

Amy McKune, curator of collections, The National Museum of Toys and Miniatures.

Beth J. Parker Miller, registrar, Winterthur Museum, Garden & Library.

Elizabeth Morton, PhD, professor of art history and department chair, Wabash College, former visiting faculty curator of African art, the Snite Museum of Art, University of Notre Dame, and visiting curator of African art, Indianapolis Museum of Art at Newfields.

Gary Metzner, head of office, Sotheby's Chicago,

Luke Nikas, partner, Quinn Emanuel Urquhart and Sullivan LLP, New York, Co-Chair, Art Litigation and Disputes.

Jeffrey H. Patchen, DME, president and CEO, The Children's Museum of Indianapolis and formerly senior program officer, the J. Paul Getty Trust.

David M. Roche, Dickey Family Director and CEO, the Heard Museum, Phoenix, Arizona.

Maaren A. Shah, partner, Quinn, Emanuel Urquhart and Sullivan LLP, New York, Co-Chair, Art Litigation Disputes..

Robert Simon, PhD, Robert Simon Fine Art, New York. European works of art from the Renaissance to the Baroque periods.

Ronald D. Spencer, attorney, Carter Ledyard & Milburn LLP, NY editor. *The Expert versus the Object: Judging Fakes and False Attributions in the Visual Arts*, Oxford University Press.

Romy M. Vreeland, former Office of the Senior Vice President, Secretary and General Counsel, The Metropolitan Museum of Art, former manager, Board of Trustees and General Counsel's office.

Laurette McCarthy, PhD; Amy McKune; Beth J. Parker Miller; Elizabeth Morton, PhD; and Romy M. Vreeland contributed substantial portions of the text.

Introduction

MUSEUMS IN THE UNITED STATES, and the public they serve, benefit immensely from the generosity of donors. The tax incentives available to those who give art, historic objects, and many other types of collectible material to qualified not-for-profit institutions encourage this philanthropy.

The synergetic relationship between donor and museum has built many invaluable museum collections over the decades, from Paul Mellon's famous "gift to the nation" that established the National Gallery of Art in the 1930s to George Gustav Heye's collection of Native American material to the National Museum of the American Indian, New York, the modernist art of Dominique and John de Menil to the Houston Museum of Fine Arts and The Menil Collections and Campus, Houston, the Walt Disney–Tishman Collection to the National Museum of African Art, Smithsonian Institution, and countless others. It is not an exaggeration to state that without the vital partnership between donors and museums, many museums in this country could not sustain their operations.

This book replaces AAM's 2011 *To Give and To Receive: A Handbook on Gifts and Donations for Museums and Donors*, whose purposes were to inform readers of then recent changes in tax law and the implications for donors and museums. The 2020 handbook format follows the process of substantiating the value of a gift and addresses the obligations of the donor and donee.

This 2020 edition also includes new case notes by Helen Harrison, Luke Nikas and Maaren Shah, Jeffrey Patchen, and Robert Simon along with Elizabeth Morton's updated section on cultural patrimony and MacKenzie Mallon's contribution on provenance. These additions focus on perspectives in collection management, provenance research, due diligence, cultural patrimony, and legal issues related to gifts to museums.

The Pension Protection Act of 2006, which was signed August 17, 2006, included key provisions that affect charitable giving and charitable donations; for this and the 2019 and 2020 update of relevant IRS publications as well as other reasons, a new publication was in order. Recent changes in IRS regulations were enacted in 2014 (IRS 8283 Non Cash Charitable Contributions), and revised IRS definitions of the standards for qualified appraisal and qualified appraiser and the mandated appraiser declaration became effective January 1, 2019.

The purpose of this 2020 edition of *To Give and To Receive: A Handbook on Collection Gifts and Donations for Museums and Donors* is to guide museums and donors through the gift process, current standards and best practices, ethical and legal issues, and IRS updates and valuation considerations, as well as to provide new case notes by museum, gallery, university, and legal professionals to emphasize collection, cultural patrimony, provenance, and copyright issues. We believe that this edition's more comprehensive approach with case studies will be useful to museums, donors, universities, foundations, and others involved in the process of giving and receiving gifts and donations.

Part One
The Museum's Perspective

CHAPTER 1

Museums as Donees
Standards, Best Practices, and Ethical and Legal Responsibilities

BETH J. PARKER MILLER and AMY MCKUNE

Obligations of the Museum as Donee

With the benefits of charitable donation come mutual obligations for both donor and museum. Nonprofit museums must follow both ethical and legal requirements in their role as a charitable organization benefiting from gifts. Museum industry best practices require museum staff and boards to consider key questions when deciding whether to accept a gift offer.

- Does the gift support the mission of the museum? Will it be useful for exhibition, educational, or research purposes?

- Can the museum legally, ethically, and effectively manage, document, care for, and use the gift?

- Can valid and unencumbered title pass to the museum? Can the gift be acquired legally? Does the donor have clear title and the legal right to make the gift? What rights will be conveyed with the gift? Is the gift unrestricted? If restricted, do the restrictions permit the museum to make best use of the object now and in the future?

- Is the object authentic? What is the provenance of the gift?

Museum collections management policies and collecting plans should guide museum decisions regarding the acceptance of a gift offer. Collections policies and plans address these and other key topics:

- What collections does the museum hold?

- What kinds of objects does the museum collect?

- What decision-making process, including legal and ethical considerations, does the museum follow to accept gifts to collections?

Title Transfer and the Museum's Role

There are three legal requirements to complete a gift: the offer (expression of intent by the donor), the acceptance by the donee, and the delivery (transfer of physical possession to the donee). The date of transfer is the date of acceptance or delivery, whichever occurs last. Documentation is a fourth important step, as the museum as the donee has the burden of proof to demonstrate that these requirements have been met. Thus, the museum must obtain and retain sufficient documentation of the transfer of title and completion of the gift.

THE OFFER

- A donor must express intent to complete the gift, whether verbally, with a letter or email communication, or through signature on a deed of gift.

- It is important at this stage of the gifting process for the museum and donor to begin discussing donor and museum intent, including use of the object, method of giving, restrictions, appraisal and tax deductions, and the museum's process and timetable for internal review and acceptance.

- Written documentation of the donor's offer should be maintained as part of the object's donation record. A countersigned deed of gift is the preferred instrument to demonstrate donor intent.

THE ACCEPTANCE

- The museum should formally accept a gift, and it is best practice to document this acceptance with a letter from the proper museum authority and a countersigned deed of gift.

- A museum's collections management policy typically addresses the process for review and acceptance of gift offers. A gift offer is commonly first entertained and evaluated at the curatorial level, with recommendations then forwarded for approval to a staff-level committee, the director or CEO, and, if

Practical Advice: Museum Stewardship of Collections

The distinctive character of museum ethics derives from the ownership, care, and use of objects, specimens and living collections representing the world's natural and cultural common wealth.

This stewardship of collections entails the highest public trust and carries with it the presumption of rightful ownership, permanence, care, documentation, accessibility and responsible disposal.

Thus, the museum ensures that: collections in its custody support its mission and public trust responsibilities; collections in its custody are lawfully held, protected, secure, unencumbered, cared for and preserved.

Elizabeth Merritt, ed. *National Standards & Best Practices for U.S. Museums*. Washington, DC: AAM Press, 2008, p. 27.

It is imperative that museum personnel strive to follow all legal and ethical standards regarding accepting gifts for the collection. The first steps in complying with these standards are to understand the legal process in which you are engaged and to accurately and effectively communicate with donors. Having policies governing these gifts, and adhering to them, is crucial.

A museum should never accept a donation that does not fit within its mission statement and the scope of the museum's collection. Having a strong collections management policy and defined scope of the collection helps guide museum personnel on making appropriate decisions about what to collect. On occasion, museum staff or board members may advocate accepting a gift as a goodwill gesture in the belief that this will prompt the donor to give future gifts that may be more desirable and appropriate for the museum. A museum should never accept a donation with the intent to deaccession it later. When museums choose to accept inappropriate gifts, they lose credibility with donors and burden themselves with the obligation to care for objects that do not serve their mission.

required by policy, the board-level collections committee and the full board of trustees. It is during this approval process that a museum should thoughtfully determine, justify, and document its reasons for accepting a gift.

- The museum's official acceptance date is determined by the institution's collections policy, and this should be applied consistently with all gifts. Some institutions consider the date of acceptance to be the date of the final step in their internal gift-approval process, documented through meeting minutes or an internal gift-approval form. Other institutions use the date of counter-signature on the deed of gift and/or letter of acceptance to the donor as the formal date of acceptance.

- Communication with the donor regarding the museum's formal acceptance of the gift is best documented in writing and should be maintained as part of the object's donation record.

THE DELIVERY

A museum as donee must take physical possession of the objects in order to complete the gift. Physical possession may be completed by an agent for the museum, such as a fine arts transportation or storage company. If the gift is a fractional interest donation, then under current law, the museum must retain substantial possession of the object.

Physical possession often precedes the acceptance, as museums frequently receive gift offers on temporary receipt so that staff may review and evaluate the objects before deciding whether to accept the donation.

Museums commonly document delivery through a receipt form, signed and dated by both parties (or their agents). These receipt documents should be maintained in the object's donation record.

Documentation

Museums and donors are best served when all steps of the gift process are documented in writing. Written documentation establishes completion dates necessary for donor tax purposes, helps prevent misunderstandings between

Practical Advice: Museum Staff Roles and Responsibilities

In accepting donations of art and objects for its collection, museum staff and board members accept a responsibility for appropriately managing these acquisitions. Museum personnel should not make promises to donors that are inconsistent with or contrary to the museum's collections management policy. For example, staff members should not promise that an object will be on permanent display.

In most cases, long-term exhibition is detrimental to the proper care of museum objects. When donors request restrictions on the gift, museum personnel must clearly communicate the museum's purpose in acquiring the object and any policy it has regarding accepting gifts with restrictions. Most museums' gift policies prohibit accepting restricted gifts.

Donors and museum personnel should clearly discuss the date of physical transfer of the gift, and the museum should take possession of the object at least by the time the gift has been completed and a signed deed of gift has been executed. If the gift spans multiple years, museum staff members need to work with the donor to pick up or receive the objects by the date of gift for each year.

In the case of fractional gifts, the museum must take substantial possession over the course of the period of the gift. The museum should consult its legal advisers regarding what constitutes "substantial possession." Museum staff should work with donors from the inception of the fractional gift (the first fractional donation) to ensure that all parties understand this provision and agree on how this obligation will be met.

Museums need a clearly defined policy of how the date of donations is determined. This is often the date that the governing board votes to accept the gift, but depending on the museum's policy, it can be another date. Donors may request that the date be adjusted to fit within IRS guidelines, for example, so that the appraisal is not dated more than sixty days before the gift. Museum staff should never change the gift date at the donor's request. From their initial contact with the donor, staff should clearly communicate the museum's process and timeline in order to allow the donor to follow IRS guidelines.

donors and museums, and enables the museum to fully document title transfer in its records. Museums need to understand that the date of donation can affect when a donor secures an appraisal and when the donor may claim a deduction.

A countersigned deed of gift, or other legal gift agreement, is the most common and preferred method of documenting the completion of a gift. Deeds of gift should

- include a full description of the donated objects,
- confirm transfer of any rights that will pass with the objects,
- note any restrictions placed on the use of the gift,
- state whether any goods or services were exchanged for the gift, and
- be signed and dated by both donor and donee.

To be fully tax-deductible, gifts should be made with no significant benefit to the donor.

Charitable Contributions Appraisals, Tax Advice, and the Museum's Role

Museum best practice guidelines strongly encourage museum staff and trustees to direct donors to seek independent tax and legal counsel related to their specific gift situation. However, this does not mean that staff should operate in a vacuum with no knowledge of law pertaining to charitable contributions. Museum staff should have some understanding of donor and donee obligations for appraisals, methods of giving, and intended use of the gift.

Appraisals for tax purposes must be completed by a qualified appraiser, as defined by the IRS. Neither museum staff nor the donor may complete an appraisal for a donation, as both are party to the transaction. Appraisals must be completed no earlier than sixty days prior to completion of the gift and no later than the due date (including any extensions) of the return. It is therefore incumbent on the museum to communicate the timeline for acceptance of the gift to a prospective donor.

Tax law applicable to fractional gifts as of 2019 requires the donor to have a new appraisal completed for each donation of additional fractions. Tax law also

Practical Advice: The Museum Deed of Gift and Completion of the Gift

Whether the gift is one object or a group of objects, one deed of gift is prepared for the donation. Sometimes, donors will choose to offer the collection over two or more years. In that case, multiple deeds of gift can be prepared outlining exactly what is included in the gift for each year. Donors will need to work independently with their own legal and tax advisors to determine how to structure the donation to best suit their tax situations. At that point, they should contact the appropriate museum staff person to discuss how they would like to structure the gift. At no time should staff engage in changing deeds of gift on accepted donations to reflect a new arrangement with the donor.

Completion of the Gift. *Museum records concerning inter vivos donations [i.e., gifts made during the donor's lifetime] should note the date on which each gift is actually placed under the control of the museum, the date on which the deed of gift (or other appropriate written evidence of donative intent) is signed, and the date on which the gift is accepted by the museum. Questions can arise between the donor and the Internal Revenue Service concerning the year in which a charitable gift was made, and copies of museum records may be requested for evidence. In the eyes of the Internal Revenue Service, a gift to charity is not eligible for a tax deduction until title has passed to the charity (usually evidenced by a deed of gift or other donative evidence and evidence that the museum accepted the gift) and the donor has relinquished control over the object. Thus evidence that the museum had a deed of gift in hand on December 31 and has accepted the gift does not secure a tax deduction for the donor for that year unless the museum can also verify that the donor effectively relinquished control of the gift before the end of the year. (And vice versa, if there is evidence that the gift was in hand on December 31, the museum can be asked to document that there was in fact a deed of gift and an acceptance in that year.) A museum*

requires museums to take "substantial physical possession" of the gift and make a related use of the property. Museums must understand their obligations and should seek legal counsel when accepting fractional gifts.

Donors that elect to take a tax deduction for a charitable contribution must file IRS Form 8283. For gifts in total value over $5,000, the authorized museum representative must complete part IV, Donor Acknowledgment, on side B of the form. The museum representative who signs the form must be authorized to sign the tax returns of the organization or must be specifically authorized to sign the Form 8283 for the organization. This individual should have a clear understanding of what the donor gave, whether any restrictions were attached to the gift, whether full or partial interest in the gift was conveyed, and the intended use of the gift, in order to accurately complete and sign the form for the museum.

Whether a gift is accepted for a related or unrelated use affects the extent of the tax deduction a donor may claim. Therefore, museums must accurately state and convey to the donor the institution's intended use of the gift. Gifts to be used for mission-related activities are usually considered "related" gifts. However, gifts of objects not related to the mission of the institution may be "unrelated." Of note, the gift of objects to a museum for the institution to sell, even if the proceeds are to benefit the collections, is considered by the IRS to be "unrelated."

Practical Advice

Appraisal Requirements

The appraisal must be made by a qualified appraiser in accordance with generally accepted appraisal standards. It also must meet the relevant requirements of IRS Regulations section 170(f)(11)(E)(i)(11) and the revised definition of the term qualified appraisal to mean an appraisal conducted by a qualified appraiser in accordance with generally accepted appraisal standards. Generally accaepted appraisal standards are defined in the regulations at I.170A-17(a)(2) as the "substance and principles of the Uniform Standards of Professional Appraisal Practice (USPAD)." The standards are developed by the Appraisal Standards Board of the Appraisal Foundation. A new declaration is also required. For further information consult I.170A-17 and www.irs.gov/irb/2006-16.

The appraisal must be made not earlier than sixty days before the date you contribute the property. You must receive the appraisal before the due date (including extensions) of the tax return on which you first claim a deduction for the property. For a deduction first claimed on an amended return, the appraisal must be received before the date the amended return was filed (Instructions for Form 8283, Noncash Charitable Contributions, Internal Revenue Service, Rev. November 2019).

As a party to the transaction, museum staff members are not permitted to perform appraisals or suggest a value to the donor. Often, donors request some help in identifying an appraiser. Many museums provide a list of appraisers or appraisal organizations that specialize in the type of objects that the museum collects. This document may include information on the process of selecting an appraiser, but museum staff should clearly communicate that they are not in a position to recommend an appraiser. The museum's role in the appraisal should be limited to making the gift available to the donor's appraiser and signing part IV, side B of IRS Form 8283.

Above all else, if ever you are asked to deviate from generally accepted practices, consult museum colleagues with a greater level of experience and/or legal counsel before proceeding.

Conclusion

Museums are stewards of collections held in trust for the public. When engaged in the charitable gifting process, museums are wise to be mindful of this role and to act not only legally but also ethically.

> Museums are expected to plan strategically and act ethically with respect to collections stewardship matters; legally, ethically, and responsibly acquire, manage, and dispose of collection items as well as know what collections are in its ownership/custody, where they came from, why it has them, and their current condition and location; and provide regular and reasonable access to, and use of, the collections/objects in its custody.

> Merritt, Elizabeth, ed. *National Standards and Best Practices for U. S. Museums*, Washington, DC: The AAM Press, American Association of Museums, 2008, p. 46.

CHAPTER 2

Gifts That Transcend Their Original Intent

The New National Art Museum of Sport at The Children's Museum of Indianapolis

JEFFREY H. PATCHEN

WHEN THE CHILDREN'S MUSEUM OF INDIANAPOLIS received a call from the board chair of the National Art Museum of Sport (NAMOS) in 2016, The Children's Museum was already planning the new 7.5-acre indoor/outdoor Riley Children's Health Sports Legends Experience, designed to inspire children and families to participate in and enjoy sports and fitness throughout their lifetimes. The project included a 13,000-square-foot indoor exhibit space—the Efroymson Pavilion—which would feature both permanent and temporary exhibits related to the world of sports.

Now the NAMOS board was offering a chance to expand the pavilion (already under construction) to include an additional dedicated space for an extraordinary collection of fine art focused on the world of sports.

The Children's Museum board agreed with its CEO and management team that an additional 3,000-square-foot permanent home for NAMOS and its collection would be a wonderful asset for the museum and for the city of Indianapolis. It would bring the arts and humanities to the world of sports and provide a unique context for understanding how a gift of art can capture individuals, teams, and special moments of emotion and inspiration.

Created in 1959 by athlete-artist Germain G. Glidden and a group of likeminded individuals, NAMOS was first housed inside the newly constructed Madison Square Garden. NAMOS relocated from the East Coast to

Indianapolis in 1991 and became an extension of Indianapolis's burgeoning sports community, first in the Bank One Tower downtown, then on the campus of Indiana University–Purdue University Indianapolis (IUPUI), and later to the National Collegiate Athletic Association (NCAA) at their national headquarters in Indianapolis.

NAMOS's Inspiration

During its fifty-three-year history, NAMOS has produced more than 100 exhibitions, including several international exhibitions at various Olympiads. Artists featured in the collection include Winslow Homer, George Bellows, LeRoy Neiman, Donald Moss, Thomas Eakins, Erté, and Muhammad Ali. By 2018, the collection consisted of 1,080 works, including 172 paintings; 111 sculptures; 274 engravings, lithographs, and serigraphs; 76 drawings; 69 photographs; 357 prints and posters; and 21 other media.

Changing space needs at IUPUI forced NAMOS to put its collection into storage in 2012 at the NCAA headquarters building not far from the IUPUI campus.

The NAMOS board conducted a nationwide search for the museum's next home and decided two things: First, NAMOS would cease operations as a stand-alone museum. Second, the collection would remain in Indianapolis.

As the largest museum of its type in the world, The Children's Museum of Indianapolis attracts nearly 1.3 million visitors each year and is among North America's top twenty-five most-visited museums. Visitors come to explore exhibits spanning the arts, sciences, and humanities. With the addition of the new Riley Children's Health Sports Legends Experience, a new permanent home for NAMOS would provide a special focus on the ability of sports to engage and inspire visitors physically, intellectually, socially, and emotionally.

By donating the entire 1,080-piece NAMOS collection to The Children's Museum, which already owned more than 130,000 cultural artifacts, natural specimens, and works of art, the NAMOS board ensured its museum collection would live on even as the founding organization ceased to exist.

With NAMOS's cooperation, The Children's Museum had the collection appraised and evaluated, not only for its insurance value but more importantly for its connection and relevance to the museum's larger Riley Children's Health Sports Legends Experience. Not surprisingly, the content of the NAMOS collection revealed extensive connections to important aspects of sport, art, and the humanities. Rich connections to a host of meaningful themes emerged, resulting in units of study for K–9 students and their teachers. Dr. Marilyn Stewart and Dr. Amy Bloom of Kutztown University of Pennsylvania assisted the museum in creating immersive units of study. The themes for the units are reflected in their titles.

- What Is Sports Art? Making a Research Sketchbook

- Who Are the Players? What Portraits Can Tell Us, Creating a Portrait

- Athletes in Action, Bodies in Motion: Seeing, Drawing, and Sculpting Bodies and Athletes in Motion, How Artists Communicate Energy, Excitement, and Speed

- Artists Set the Stage, Places in Sports: Considering Place and Space, Mapping and Making Places for Sports

- Looking Back in Time: Learning about the Past from Works of Art, Games of the Past

Reimaging NAMOS

From the beginning, the 7.5-acre Riley Children's Health Sports Legends Experience had an ambitious goal. At a time when both adult and childhood obesity rates were climbing, the museum wanted to create a family learning experience in spaces that encouraged and inspired children and adults to get fit together by taking part in sports and having fun.

To create opportunities for encouragement and inspiration, the museum wanted to expose children to some of Indiana's greatest sports legends—men and women whose accomplishments made them role models both as athletes and as human beings.

This was the basis to commission twelve bronze statues by sculptor Brian Cooley to line a proposed Avenue of Champions throughout the outdoor sports experience. These twelve sculptures included basketball legends Larry Bird, Tamika Catchings, Bobby "Slick" Leonard, Reggie Miller, and Oscar Robertson; acclaimed Negro League Baseball Team the Indianapolis Clowns and three of its players (Henry Aaron, Mamie "Peanut" Johnson, and Tony Stone); auto racing champion A. J. Foyt Jr.; hockey great Wayne Gretzky; race ace Wilma Rudolph; the Indianapolis Colts' record-setting Reggie Wayne; and tennis advocate Barbara Wynne. The twelve sculptures were accessioned into the NAMOS collection.

The Children's Museum raised an additional $3.5 million above and beyond the $35 million required for the Riley Children's Health Sports Legends Experience to cover the costs of the pavilion expansion for NAMOS and to endow both a full-time staff position and programming. Selections from the NAMOS collection would be the basis for permanent and temporary exhibitions in the new National Art Museum of Sport for years to come. In addition, the museum introduced its first endowed visiting artist program, a project of the Lechleiter Indiana Visiting Artist Fund at The Children's Museum, featuring NAMOS artist C. W. Mundy. The artist's twenty-four presentations in the NAMOS gallery have successfully immersed families and school groups in art making and art history.

In March 2018, the new National Art Museum of Sport, presented by the George and Peggy Rapp Family, and an accompanying Special Exhibit Gallery, presented by Ice Miller Legal Counsel, opened in the Efroymson Pavilion of the Riley Children's Health Sports Legends Experience at The Children's Museum of Indianapolis. The museum also created and debuted a new interactive database of the NAMOS collection that can be searched by artist, medium, subject, or date. Just before the opening, the LeRoy Neiman Foundation donated 268 prints and drawings by the artist, which also became part of the NAMOS collection.

The reimagined NAMOS is designed as a visitor-centered, family-centered gallery with a variety of family learning activities to engage children, their parents, and their grandparents and includes a special art-making studio space.

In addition, the museum's professional actor–interpreters engage visitors to the gallery and provide important historical and cultural context for the works and the moments in time they represent. The goal for the new NAMOS is to share with visitors the best in sports-related fine art while also inspiring them to create their own works.

The gift of the NAMOS collection to The Children's Museum of Indianapolis provided an extraordinary opportunity to leverage an important and meaningful collection of fine art. More importantly, this collection will reach millions of children and their families for decades to come. It is truly a museum gift that transcends the original intent to become the new National Art Museum of Sport at The Children's Museum of Indianapolis.

CHAPTER 3

Donation Process and Procedure Outline

ROMY M. VREELAND

IT IS IMPORTANT FOR INSTITUTIONS that accept gifts of property to have a written donation procedure outline available for their staff and for potential donors. The outline may incorporate the institution's specific mission and collecting strategy, its policies for accepting donations of property, applicable IRS rules and other statutes that may have bearing on tax deductions and the transfer of title, and the types of donor recognition offered by the institution.

If a donor understands an institution's gift acceptance policies and timeline (which may differ from that of other institutions a donor has dealt with), major problems can be avoided. Evidence of a clearly worded and thoughtfully prepared procedure will instill confidence in a donor and convey that the same institutional standards apply to all gifts of property to the institution.

Likewise, having a plainly worded procedure available to all staff who have a hand in soliciting donations of property (who may include an institution's director, board members, development team, researchers, and educators, as well as curators) will help the staff present a consistent and accurate message to donors, avoiding misunderstandings down the line when they are more difficult to correct. The procedure should be based on the policies contained in an institution's collection-management policy, by-laws, or other governing documents. Having a document tailored to answer a donor's questions about the giving process, and making certain that the document is in plain language, may be more helpful than presenting your governing documents to a potential donor.

The procedure should not take the place of a donor's consultation with his or her own financial, legal, or tax advisers, but it can help the donor open a discussion with his or her adviser and can help the adviser better understand your institution's own specific policies and motivations.

The following points should be considered by an institution as it crafts its donation procedure or revisits its donation acceptance process and can guide a donor to ask the right questions of an institution that does not have a complete or accessible written policy. Note that the outline is meant to be just that: a simple statement of policy that can help guide decision making and not a comprehensive document that attempts to illustrate all possible gift transactions and potential issues.

- Introduce your institution's mission, and note the type and range of objects or other works your institution collects. Explain why donations are an important part of your collections-building strategy.

- Explain how a dialogue is opened about a potential gift. Note who in the organization normally makes the initial contact with a donor, and why.

- Outline the normal flow of paperwork when an offered gift is of interest to the institution, when the property considered for donation is expected to arrive at the institution, and who in the institution will handle physical receipt of the property.

- If your institution has a policy on restrictive terms, or on different types of giving, such as promised and partial interest gifts, explain that policy. It may be helpful to note that any gift other than an outright, unrestricted gift of property may reduce the level of the gift's tax deductibility and should be discussed with a financial adviser before proceeding. Likewise, you may wish to explain the concept of unrelated use (see chapter 28, "Related and Unrelated Use" in this handbook for more information) and state your institution's policy on accepting gifts for an unrelated use, such as sale at a fund-raising auction.

- Explain the value of bequests and any special services or recognition your institution may offer for planned giving. Stress that planned gifts should be discussed with the donor's legal and financial advisers.

- Note the ways in which your institution recognizes gifts of property, such as in credit lines, the annual report or newsletters, complimentary memberships, private tours or events, and the like.

- Explain how your institution handles requests for appraisals and tax documentation and what types of documents are automatically provided to the donor. It is an excellent idea to state that appraisals for tax purposes cannot be provided by a donee institution under IRS rules.

- Include any links or references to helpful information pertinent to your donors, such as a special section of your website about gifts and fund-raising, published information about past gifts accepted by your institution, or the names of useful IRS publications and forms.

- Include contact information for any person or department mentioned in your outline.

This is a guide to help you begin to think about the policies and procedures that are important to your donors. Your outline will vary depending on whether it will be used primarily for sharing with donors, for staff instruction, or both. Please see the following chapter for an excerpt from the brochure "Gifts of Works of Art" published by The Metropolitan Museum of Art as an example of an outline to be supplied to potential donors.

CHAPTER 4

Gifts of Works of Art Brochure

THE METROPOLITAN MUSEUM OF ART

Gifts of Art

SINCE ITS INCEPTION IN 1870, The Metropolitan Museum of Art has relied on the support of friends to amass a collection of artistic treasures spanning five thousand years of world culture. Donors of gifts of art to the Museum will join an illustrious group of those who have, with their gifts and personal dedication, built the Museum into the foremost art institution in the Western Hemisphere and the most encyclopedic museum in the world. The Museum depends on the continued commitment of its donors to preserve its educational mission and maintain its ability to serve the public.

Over the years, federal, state, and local governments have encouraged private philanthropy through favorable tax laws. Significant tax incentives exist for those who give art, cash, or securities to qualified not-for-profit institutions like the Metropolitan Museum.

This brochure provides general information to those individuals considering the donation of a gift of art to the Museum. However, in the course of planning a gift, you should consult with your attorney or tax adviser to determine the best gift arrangement for your particular situation.

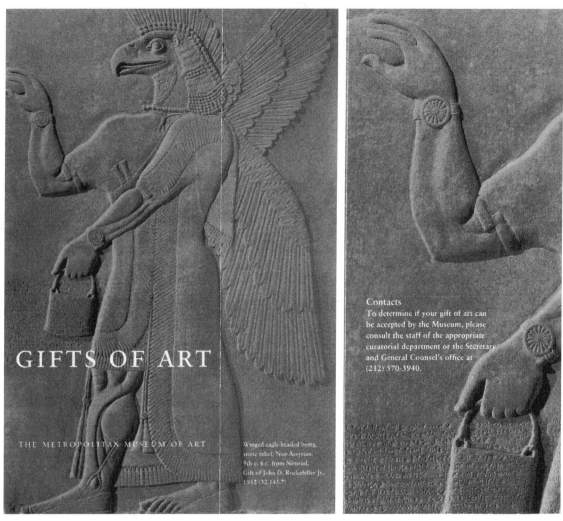

Figure 4.1. Gifts of Art brochure. The Metropolitan Museum of Art

GIFTS OF ART TO BENEFIT THE MUSEUM NOW

OUTRIGHT GIFT OF A WORK OF ART

Traditionally, donors have been motivated to give art, such as paintings, sculptures, or furniture, to the Metropolitan Museum out of personal concern for the arts and an interest in furthering appreciation of art in New York City and in the nation. Your outright donation of art to the Metropolitan will benefit the

Museum by making the object a part of the collection and available for immediate use.

In addition, your donation of art entitles you to an income tax deduction. An object that has appreciated in value and has been held for at least twelve months prior to donation may entitle you to a charitable deduction equal to the fair market value of the object.

You should be aware that the charitable income tax deduction available for gifts of art that have appreciated in value is generally available in an amount up to 30% of your adjusted gross income for that year. A gift in excess of that limit may be carried forward as a deduction against income for up to five years.

PARTIAL INTEREST GIFTS

A partial interest gift is a gift of an undivided fractional interest in a particular work of art. Partial interest gifts have been the subject of recent changes in the law. It is important that you consult with your tax advisor before proceeding with a partial interest gift. Should you wish to proceed, you are entitled to an immediate charitable deduction equal to the lesser of the value of the work at the time of your initial fractional contribution or the value of the work at the time of any additional contribution. For example, a donor whose painting is worth $1 million in the first year the donor makes a fractional gift bases the tax deduction on a percentage of the $1 million valuation. If, five years later, when the donor gives another fraction, the painting is worth $2 million, the donor must use the $1 million valuation. Under current law, 100 percent of the gift must be transferred within ten years of the initial fractional contribution or the death of the donor, whichever is first. During the ten-year period, the Museum must have substantial physical possession of the work as long as the donor remains alive.

LOANS

You may decide to lend art to the Museum for an indefinite time period. No tax deduction is available for a loan because no gift has been made.

GIFTS FOR THE FUTURE

PROMISED GIFTS

You may wish to commit to giving a work of art to the Museum at a later date by signing a promised gift agreement. If the gift is not completed during your lifetime, the art will come to the Museum upon your death. A promised gift agreement is a binding obligation and is not revocable. There is no tax deduction, however, until title and possession of the art is given in whole or in part to the Museum.

BEQUESTS

You may choose to leave art to the Museum in your will. In such a case, you retain complete interest in the art with the freedom to sell or transfer it elsewhere during your lifetime. If the art remains in your possession, it will pass to the Museum at your death, and your estate will receive an estate tax charitable deduction for its full market value.

THE WILLIAM SOCIETY

Providing for a future gift to the Museum either by a promised gift agreement or in your will makes you eligible for membership in the William Society.

ADDITIONAL INFORMATION

APPRAISALS

If you claim a deduction for a gift of art in excess of $5,000 you must obtain a qualified appraisal of the value of the art before you file your tax return. The Museum is prohibited by law from providing appraisals, but at your request the appropriate curatorial department would be happy to provide a list of possible appraisers.

The appraisal cannot be made more than sixty days before the date of contribution but must be completed before you file your tax return.

The cost of obtaining the appraisal is your sole responsibility and is not allowable as a charitable deduction. It may be deductible as a miscellaneous expense.

Your claim for an income tax charitable deduction must be accompanied by IRS Form 8283, which contains a summary of the appraisal as well as the signature of the Museum's secretary acknowledging the contribution. For gifts of art valued at $20,000 or more (in the aggregate) you must submit a copy of the full appraisal with your tax return.

Part Two
The Donor's Perspective

CHAPTER 5

Responsibilities of the Donor

ROMY M. VREELAND

THERE ARE MANY REASONS for a donor to offer an object of value to a museum, and these range from pure philanthropy and a desire to serve the community to the financial purpose of receiving a tax deduction. Whatever the intention behind the gift, the donor should be fully aware of the legal, ethical, and financial responsibilities that a gift of property to a museum entails. And it is of the utmost importance for the donor to know as much as possible about the museum, its expectations and requirements as recipient, and its plans for how the gift not only relates to its collections but will also be acknowledged, cared for, and displayed. This section of the book helps guide the donor through the process.

When making a gift to a museum, the donor should always

- clearly understand the museum's intended use for the donation;

- make clear the donor's own intentions;

- secure a qualified appraisal of the gift if the total value is more than $5,000;

- arrange the transfer of possession, title, and rights, typically through a deed of gift;

- prepare documentation of ownership, provenance, and significance of times and dates; and

- discuss with the museum any restrictions on the gift.

CHAPTER 6
Donations to Museums
An Overview

ROMY M. VREELAND

WITH ANY GIFT OF PROPERTY TO A MUSEUM, whether a painting, a historical artifact, ceramics, textiles, or even a gift of stock or real estate, we begin by determining the fair market value of the gift. This is essential when the donor intends to seek a tax deduction for a charitable gift.

Fair market value (FMV) is the price that an item would sell for on the open market. It is the price that would be agreed on between a willing buyer and a willing seller, with neither being required to act and both having reasonable knowledge of the relevant facts. If you put a restriction on the use of the item you donate—for example, that it must be exhibited annually or cannot be sold—the FMV could be affected by that restriction.

Fair market value relates to a range of gifts to museums, including both planned gifts and fractional gifts, discussed later in this book.

According to IRS Publication 561, Determining the Value of Property, there are four factors to consider in researching the market to estimate value. Here, "property" also refers to an object or artifact and not only or specifically to real estate.

1. Cost or Selling Price of the Property. The cost or selling price of the property may be a good indication of the property's fair market value depending on the following:

  a. The purchase or sale date was reasonably close to the date of contribution.

  b. Any decrease or increase in value, compared to your cost, is calculated at a reasonable rate.

c. The terms of purchase or sale do not limit what can be done with the property.

d. There was no "arm's length" offer—a transaction in which the parties involved act independently of each other and in their own self-interest—to buy the property close to the valuation date.

2. Sales of Comparable Property. The sale of properties similar to the donated property is often important in determining FMV. The weight to be given to each sale depends on the following:

a. How similar is the property sold to the property donated?

b. How close is the date of sale to the valuation date?

c. Was the sale at "arm's length"?

d. What was the condition of the market at the time of sale?

3. Replacement Cost. The replacement cost is the amount it would cost to replace the donated item as of the valuation date. Often there may be a limited relationship between the replacement cost and the FMV.

a. What would it cost to replace the donated property?

b. Is there a reasonable relationship between the replacement cost and the fair market value?

c. Is the supply of the donated property more or less than the demand for it?

4. Opinion of Experts.

a. Is the expert knowledgeable and competent?

b. Is the opinion thorough and supported by facts and experience?

IF the factor you are considering is . . .	THEN you should ask these questions...
cost or selling price	Was the purchase or sale of the property reasonably close to the date of contribution? Was an increase or decrease in value, as compared to your cost, at a reasonable rate? Do the terms of purchase or sale limit what can be done with the property? Was there an arm's-length offer to buy the property close to the valuation date?
sales of comparable properties	How similar is the property sold to the property donated? How close is the date of sale to the valuation date? Was the sale at arm's length? What was the condition of the market at the time of sale?
replacement cost	What would it cost to replace the donated property? Is there a reasonable relationship between replacement cost and FMV? Is the supply of the donated property more or less than the demand for it?
opinions of experts	Is the expert knowledgeable and competent? Is the opinion thorough and supported by facts and experience?

The Compliance Process

Gifts of property should be understood within the context of the requirements for all charitable deductions. Regardless of the type of object, contributions of $5,000 or more to a charitable organization must be substantiated by submitting a complete appraisal document that adheres to IRS requirements.

For most types of objects valued at over $5,000, an appraisal should be obtained for the donor's records and used to complete the required information on IRS Form 8283. For works of art valued at $20,000 or more, the appraisal must also be submitted with the tax return.

Types of Donations

According to IRS Publication 561, the requirement for an appraisal applies to any donation that meets both of the following criteria:

1. It is a gift of property (objects and materials, nonpublicly traded stock, and real estate).

2. The value of an individual item or of a group of similar items exceeds $5,000, or, in the case of closely held stock, exceeds $10,000.

This requirement does not apply to donations of cash or publicly traded securities.

Deductions

Generally, a tax deduction is allowed based on the full FMV of tangible personal property that

- is long-term capital gain property owned for more than one year,
- is contributed to a qualified organization,
- satisfies the related use rule, and
- has a qualified appraisal by a qualified appraiser (when applicable).

There are exceptions to fair market deduction, however, that may limit the deduction to cost basis.

Related Use Property

In order for the donor to receive the maximum allowable tax deduction, the use of the property by the donee (nonprofit) organization must be related to the purpose or function of the organization's tax exemption. If the donee wishes to use the donated property for an unrelated use (e.g., to be sold in a charity auction to raise funds for the institution's mission), this should be discussed with the donor before the gift is made. If property accepted as related use is put to an unrelated use by the donee within three years of its receipt as a gift, the donee must file Form 8282 with the IRS, and this could affect the donor's tax liability.

Limitations and Reductions

Any asset can be considered ordinary income property or capital gain property, depending on the circumstances. The federal tax code and the characterization of the property by its owner determine whether an exchange or transfer of the property results in ordinary income or a capital gain. The tax treatment of a gain from the sale of any given property depends on the length of time and the purpose for which the property is held.

Examples of ordinary income property include

- inventory,
- property created by donor, for example, the artist (who can claim a deduction for the cost of materials only),
- property received by donor as a gift from the creator (i.e., the artist), and
- property held for less than one year.

Generally, donating any of these types of property limits deduction to a cost basis—that is, the cost paid for the property.

IRS Publication 526: Charitable Contributions (available at www.irs.gov) explains how to claim a deduction for your charitable contributions. It discusses

- organizations that are qualified to receive deductible charitable contributions,

- the types of contributions you can deduct,

- how much you can deduct,

- what records to keep, and

- how to report charitable contributions.

If you give property to a qualified organization, you can generally deduct the fair market value of the property at the time of the contribution.

Your deduction for charitable contributions is generally limited to 50 percent of your adjusted gross income, but in some cases 20 percent and 30 percent limits may apply. In addition, the total of your charitable contributions deduction and certain other itemized deductions may be limited. Donors should consult a qualified accountant, certified public accountant, or financial planner on these matters.

CHAPTER 7

Donor Record Keeping and Reporting
Sample Deed of Gift

AMY MCKUNE, BETH J. PARKER MILLER, and ROMY M. VREELAND

THE DEED OF GIFT IS OF PRIMARY IMPORTANCE. This document is prepared by the museum and must make clear the process through which the title and ownership are transferred and the effective date of the transfer of ownership.

SAMPLE: DEED OF GIFT

I (We) hereby irrevocably and unconditionally give, transfer, and assign to the [institution] all of my (our) right, title, and interests in, to, and associated with the object(s) described below, including, but not limited to, all applicable copyright, trademark, and related interests. I (We) affirm that I (we) lawfully own said object(s) and possess full authority to transfer good title to it, free of any other claims.

[Description of object(s)]

Signature of donor(s) _____

Please print name(s) _____

Dated this _____ day of _____ , _____

I/(We) wish to designate the following the credit line (optional):

_____

(Donors wishing to remain anonymous may enter "anonymous" on the line above. If no credit line is specified, your name as signed above will be used.)

ACKNOWLEDGMENT OF ACCEPTANCE

[Institution] hereby gratefully acknowledges receipt of the gift of property as described in the above Deed of Gift on this _____ day of _____ , _____ .

Signed: _____
    [Name of officer], [Title of officer], on behalf of [institution]

CHAPTER 8
Caveat Mutuor
A Cautionary Tale

HELEN A. HARRISON

IN THE SPRING OF 2003, the artist and art collector Arthur Byron Phillips, a Scranton, Pennsylvania, native who had a long association with the city's Everhart Museum of Natural History Science and Art,[1] offered to lend the museum a painting he said he had purchased directly from Jackson Pollock. The museum accepted, and no one questioned its bona fides.

The 32-by-40-inch canvas, signed and dated "Jackson Pollock 49," lower right, was given the title *Springs Winter*[2] by Phillips, Springs being the eastern Long Island hamlet in the town of East Hampton, New York, where Pollock and his wife, the artist Lee Krasner, lived and worked. Evidently the swirling tracery of white paint, overlying and intertwining with gray and black pourings, suggested a snowstorm to Phillips.

This would not be the only Pollock to have acquired a descriptive title after the fact. In 1948, in order to obviate literal interpretation of his abstract imagery, the artist stopped titling his paintings and started numbering them. As Krasner explained to an interviewer, "numbers are neutral." Among those that later were given names are *Autumn Rhythm*: Number 30, 1950; *Lavender Mist*: Number 1, 1950; and *Convergence*: Number 10, 1952.

According to Phillips, *Springs Winter* had hung in the family home in Scranton since his mother, Ida, bought it for him in 1951—first in his bedroom and later in the sunroom, where his niece, Jenny Mittelman, remembers seeing it when she was a teenager.[3] After Ida's death in 1999, it remained in the house, where Phillips often spent several weeks or months a year.

Figure 8.1. Jackson Pollock (1912–1956). *Springs Winter*. 1949. Oil on canvas, 32 x 40. *Photograph courtesy of the Everhart Museum.*

By that time, however, his primary residence had long been in East Hampton, and he was concerned that the Scranton house was not secure. While he had never had *Springs Winter* appraised, he believed it to be so valuable that insuring it would be prohibitively expensive.

He therefore decided to lend it anonymously to the Everhart, both to share it with the public and to give it the protection of the museum's security system and insurance coverage.

The Everhart describes itself as an interdisciplinary museum with "significant holdings in American folk art, works on paper, [and] works created by art practitioners with connections to Northeast Pennsylvania," as well as rocks, minerals, birds, plants, and Dorflinger glass—cut lead crystal ware manufactured in the late nineteenth and early twentieth century in White Mills, Pennsylvania. As noted on its website, its holdings include African, American, Asian,

European, and contemporary art, as well as design arts. These holdings span different time periods and cultures. The art collections comprise paintings, sculpture, decorative arts, prints, drawings, photographs, and textiles. Among the modern American artists represented in the collection are Alex Katz, Raphael Soyer, Robert Henri, Chaim Gross, and regional artists.

Yet despite its extensive holdings, the museum accepted *Spring Winter* even though Phillips had not obtained an appraisal, nor had he had the painting examined by the Jackson Pollock Authentication Committee, composed of Krasner and a group of leading Pollock scholars, including Francis V. O'Connor and Eugene V. Thaw, who compiled the artist's catalogue raisonné (published in four volumes by Yale University Press in 1978), or by its successor, the Pollock-Krasner Authentication Board, a panel of experts operating under the aegis of the Pollock-Krasner Foundation after Krasner's death in 1984. Following lawsuits by owners of paintings it had declined to approve, the board published a Pollock catalogue raisonné supplement and ceased operations in 1995.

As a friend of Phillips, who served on the Pollock-Krasner House and Study Center's advisory committee, I urged him more than once to submit the painting to the board. He told me he was reluctant to remove it from the Scranton house and take it to New York City for examination and that in any case he felt it was unnecessary, since he wasn't planning to sell it. Moreover, he said, he knew it was genuine because he had first laid eyes on it propped against the wood stove in the Pollock-Krasner House living room.[4]

His description of its purchase was quite detailed. He said that in the summer of 1951, at age fouteen,[5] he visited East Hampton with his Scranton art teacher, Margaret Oettinger, whose sister Marian and her husband, the artist David Porter, lived in the area. The Porters were friends of Pollock, and Marion asked if Phillips would like to visit his studio. As an aspiring artist himself, he was thrilled at the opportunity to meet the painter, who had been made nationally famous by a *Life* magazine profile two years earlier.

Although his own art would go in the opposite direction from Pollock's—he became a naturalistic painter in the manner of Andrew Wyeth, to whose work his is often compared—Phillips was intrigued by the canvas leaning on the stove. He asked if it was for sale, and Pollock said yes.

Figure 8.2.   Arthur Byron Phillips (1927–2008), *Self-Portrait*. Undated. Pastel on paper, 20 x 16 inches. *Private collection.*

As Phillips told Paul Vitello of the *New York Times* in 2006, "I called my mother on the telephone and asked her to buy it. Pollock wanted $1,000. My mother haggled him down to $800."[6]

Why would the *New York Times* be talking to Phillips? Because on November 18, 2005, the painting was stolen from the Everhart Museum.

The museum's alarm sounded at 2:32 a.m., and by the time the police arrived, less than five minutes later, the thieves were gone. (Unfortunately, though the motion sensors were working, the video cameras were not.) Screened by a large tent that covered the rear entrance, installed for Saturday's annual Everhart Ball, the thieves had shattered glass doors at the back of the building. In addition to *Springs Winter*, they also took *Le Grand Passion*, a 1984 screen print by Andy Warhol. Joe Palumbo, a museum spokesperson, told the press that the thieves "knew exactly what they wanted. Nothing else was disturbed inside the museum. There was no other damage or anything else missing."[7]

The theft was reported to the Philadelphia branch of the Federal Bureau of Investigation, and claims for both stolen works were filed with Murray Insurance Agency Inc., which held the blanket policy on the museum's collections. Three months later, in February 2006, the company reported that it would reimburse the Everhart $100,000 for the missing Warhol but would not be responsible for the loss of the Pollock, which Brian J. Murray,[8] the firm's principal and a member of the Everhart's board of trustees, believed was a fake.

Murray's opinion was based on the findings of a New York City art and antiques appraisal company, which examined photographs of the painting and related documentation. While the appraisal firm did not declare the work to be fraudulent, its president and damage/loss specialist told the *Scranton Times-Tribune* that "we did not find any reason to believe it is a work by Pollock."

Phillips's account was undermined by the lack of a bill of sale, receipt, cancelled check, or any other evidence of the purchase and no history of the painting's exhibition or publication.[9] In hindsight it also seemed suspicious that he had never availed himself of the opportunity to have the painting examined by Pollock experts. He would not have been required to take it to the authentication board; he could have submitted a photograph for initial consideration. Lacking both provenance and the approval of Pollock experts, the museum's claim was rejected.

"What we first thought was a loss turned out to be nothing at all," said Murray. Had the painting been accepted as genuine, it could have been worth as much as $11.6 million, the price of Number 12, 1949, a comparable Pollock sold at Christie's New York on May 11, 2004.

Murray's findings were hotly disputed by Phillips, who not only insisted that the painting was a genuine Pollock but also gave the FBI the name of someone he suspected was the thief—someone with "a connection to the museum." That assertion was dismissed by Palumbo, who said that the Everhart's board had no reason to "believe the theft was perpetrated by anyone affiliated with the museum," and they had no idea who the thief or thieves might be.[10] Evidently Phillips's accusation led nowhere, since no one has ever been charged. The painting and the Warhol print are still listed in the FBI's stolen art database.

On the tenth anniversary of the theft, the *Times-Tribune* ran a follow-up article by David Singleton, who noted that "the crime is unsolved, the artwork unrecovered, and many questions surrounding the break-in [are] still unanswered." He summarized the most intriguing question in three words: "real or fake?"[11]

Perhaps an even more intriguing question is why the Everhart accepted *Springs Winter* at face value. Singleton quoted an official 2006 statement from the museum that defended the "good faith loan" and maintained that the jury was still out: "Until that time when [the painting] is recovered, all arguments for and against its authenticity are exercises in speculation and are a disservice to both Mr. Phillips and the Everhart." Nevertheless, since art forgers often try to place their handiwork in exhibitions and publications in order to insert them into the artist's body of work, the lack of documentation for *Springs Winter* should have raised concerns.

Consider the case of Mark Landis, the subject of the 2014 documentary *Art and Craft*, whose forgeries were accepted as donations by more than forty-five museums.[12]

Landis is described as an eccentric character who made his gifts with the implication that financial support might follow. The same could be said of Phillips, who had already arranged for the donation of two of his own works to the Everhart and was believed, correctly, to be a multimillionaire.[13]

Given Phillips's long-standing relationship with the museum, officials had a hard time believing that he would deliberately deceive them. "Arthur did a lot of odd things," Palumbo told Singleton, "but I don't think he'd just make it up. He really had no reason to."[14] Yet with nothing more than his word to go on—especially since the value of a comparable Pollock was higher than the insurance coverage of the museum's entire art collection—the risk clearly outweighed the potential reward.

Before accepting the loan, the Everhart could have had the painting appraised with a view to taking out a rider, as is normally done for loan exhibitions. If the appraisal had cast doubt on its authenticity and caused the insurer to deny coverage, the museum would have been able to decline the loan gracefully. If the rider had been approved, it would have been hard for the insurer to dismiss the claim.

The moral of the story? Borrower beware. Even when the lender is a friend.

Notes

1. Phillips had a solo exhibition at the Everhart in 1958 and again shortly before he lent *Springs Winter* to the museum, which owns two of his egg tempera paintings on panel. I am grateful to the museum's preparator, Michael Wisneski, for this and other information related to Phillips's dealings with the Everhart Museum.

2. In press reports, Phillips gave the title as *Winter in Springs*, but Michael Wisneski confirms that on the Everhart loan agreement, dated April 1, 2003, signed by Phillips, the title he supplied is *Springs Winter*.

3. Telephone interview with Jenny K. Mittelman, May 9, 2019.

4. Although there is no longer such a stove in the house, there was a Franklin stove in the back parlor when Pollock and Krasner bought the property in 1946.

5. If Phillips acquired the painting in 1951, he was in fact twenty-four years old, not fourteen.

6. Paul Vitello, "The Case of the Purloined, Unauthenticated Pollock," *New York Times*, March 14, 2006. The article contains a summary of the other news reports and the statements by Murray and Lake-Ewald as well as quotes by me regarding my efforts to persuade Phillips to have the painting reviewed by the authentication board.

7. "Warhol and Pollock Works of Art Stolen from Everhart Museum in Scranton," *Antiques and the Arts Weekly*, November 22, 2005.

8. A report in the September 11, 2011, online issue of *Insurance Journal* noted that "A former northeastern Pennsylvania insurance executive [Brian J. Murray, 68] has been sentenced to 5½ to 16½ years in state prison in what prosecutors said was a pyramid scheme worth at least $7 million." This conviction is unrelated to the Everhart theft.

9. In the 1978 Jackson Pollock catalogue raisonné, five paintings dated 1949 are documented and listed as "works which cannot be visually identified and/or located." Four were exhibited at the Betty Parsons Gallery, and one was sold through The Museum of Modern Art's Art Lending Service. None match the dimensions of *Springs Winter*.

10. Michael Rubicam, "Who Stole Jackson Pollock? Painter's Owner Gives FBI a Name," Associated Press, January 26, 2006.

11. David Singleton, "10 Years Later, Everhart Theft Remains Unsolved," *Scranton Times-Tribune*, November 18, 2014. I am grateful to Mr. Singleton for supplying several

documents related to the Phillips family and for his cooperation in the research for this essay.

12. Stephen Holden, "For This Con Artist, No Crime That Pays," *New York Times*, September 18, 2014.

13. According to Phillips's will, supplied by Singleton and confirmed by the attorney and co-executor Thomas J. Osborne of East Hampton, the estate was valued at $7 million.

14. Singleton, loc. cit.

Part Three
The IRS Perspective

compiled and edited by LAURETTE E. MCCARTHY

CHAPTER 9

Noncash Contributions over $5,000 and Records to Retain

IN FIGURING WHETHER YOUR DEDUCTION is over $5,000, combine your claimed deductions for all similar items of property donated to any charitable organization during the year.

If you make a noncash contribution of $5,000 or more, you must obtain and keep a receipt from the charitable organization showing

1. the name of the charitable organization,

2. the date and location of the charitable contribution,

3. a reasonably detailed description of the property, and

4. the donee must also obtain a qualified appraisal and complete and sign IRS Form 8283.

A letter or other written communication from the charitable organization acknowledging receipt of the contribution and containing the information in (1), (2), and (3) will serve as a receipt.

Personal Records to Retain

You must also keep reliable written records for each item of donated property. Your written records must include the following information:

1. The name and address of the organization to which you contributed.

2. The date and location of the contribution.

3. A description of the property in as much detail as is reasonable under the circumstances.

4. The fair market value of the property at the time of the contribution and how you figured the fair market value. If it was determined by appraisal, you should also keep a copy of the signed appraisal.

5. The cost or other basis of the property if you must reduce its fair market value by appreciation. Your records should also include the amount of the reduction and how you estimated it. If you choose the 50 percent limit instead of the special 30 percent limit on certain capital gain property (discussed under Capital Gain Property, p. 6, IRS Publication 561), you must keep a record showing the years for which you made the choice, contributions for the current year to which the choice applies, and carryovers from preceding years to which the choice applies.

6. The amount you claim as a deduction for the tax year as a result of the contribution, if you contribute less than your entire interest in the property during the tax year. Your records must include the amount you claimed as a deduction in any earlier years for contributions of other interests in this property. They must also include the name and address of each organization to which you contributed the other interests, the place where any such tangible property is located or kept, and the name of any person in possession of the property, other than the organization to which you contributed.

7. The terms of any conditions attached to the gift of property.

You must also secure and keep an acknowledgment of your contribution from the qualified organization. If you made more than one contribution of $5,000 or more, you must have either a separate acknowledgment for each or one acknowledgment that shows your total contributions.

The acknowledgment must also meet these tests:

1. It must be written.

2. It must include

a. a description (but not necessarily the value) of any property you contributed,

b. whether the qualified organization gave you any goods or services as a result of your contribution (other than certain token items and membership benefits), and

c. a description and good-faith estimate of the value of any goods or services described in (b). If, for example, the only benefit you received was an intangible religious benefit (such as admission to a religious ceremony) that generally is not sold in a commercial transaction outside the donative context, the acknowledgment must say so and does not need to describe or estimate the value of the benefit.

3. You must obtain the acknowledgment on or before the earlier of

a. the date you file your return for the year you make the contribution, or

b. the due date, including extensions, for filing the return.

4. Your records must also include

a. how you acquired the property—for example, by purchase, gift, bequest, inheritance, or exchange;

b. the approximate date you got the property or, if created, produced, or manufactured by or for you, the approximate date the property was substantially completed; and

c. the cost or other basis, and any adjustments to the basis, of property held less than twelve months and, if available, the cost or other basis of property held twelve months or more. This requirement, however, does not apply to publicly traded securities.

If you are not able to provide information on either the date you acquired the property or the cost basis of the property, and you have a reasonable cause for not being able to provide this information, attach a statement of explanation to your return.

Generally, you must also obtain a qualified written appraisal of the donated property from a qualified appraiser. This appraisal should not be made more than sixty days prior to the effective donation date.

CHAPTER 10

Synopsis of IRS Publication 561
Determining the Value of Donated Property

IRS PUBLICATION 561 IS DESIGNED to help donors and appraisers estimate the fair market value of property (other than cash) that is given to qualified organizations. It also explains what kind of information you must have to support the charitable contribution deduction you claim on your tax return.

This publication does not discuss how to figure the amount of your deduction for charitable contributions or written records and substantiation required. For that information, see IRS Publication 526: Charitable Contributions.

Deductions of More Than $5,000

Generally, if the claimed deduction for an item or group of similar items of donated property is more than $5,000, you must obtain a qualified appraisal made by a qualified appraiser, and you must attach section B of Form 8283 to your tax return. You should keep the appraiser's report with your written records. (Exceptions: you must attach a complete, signed copy of your appraisal for art valued at $20,000 or more and deductions of other property valued at more than $500,000.)

The phrase "similar items" means property of the same generic category or type (whether or not donated to the same donee), such as stamp collections, coin collections, lithographs, paintings, photographs, books, nonpublicly traded stock, nonpublicly traded securities other than nonpublicly traded stock, land, buildings, clothing, jewelry, furniture, electronic equipment, household appliances, toys, everyday kitchenware, china, crystal, or silver.

EXCEPTIONS

You do not need an appraisal if the property is

- nonpublicly traded stock of $10,000 or less,

- a vehicle (including a car, boat, or airplane) for which your deduction is limited to the gross proceeds from its sale,

- qualified intellectual property, such as a patent,

- certain publicly traded securities (described next),

- inventory and other property donated by a corporation that are "qualified contributions" for the care of the ill, the needy, or infants, within the meaning of section Publication 561 (April 2007) 170(e)(3)(A) of the Internal Revenue Code, or

- stock in trade, inventory, or property held primarily for sale to customers in the ordinary course of your trade or business.

Although an appraisal is not required for the types of property just listed, you must provide certain information about a donation of any of these types of property on Form 8283.

PUBLICLY TRADED SECURITIES

Even if your claimed deduction is more than $5,000, neither a qualified appraisal nor section B of Form 8283 is required for publicly traded securities that are

- listed on a stock exchange in which quotations are published on a daily basis,

- regularly traded in a national or regional over-the-counter market for which published quotations are available, or

- shares of an open-end investment company (mutual fund) for which quotations are published on a daily basis in a newspaper of general circulation throughout the United States.

Publicly traded securities that meet these requirements must be reported on Form 8283, section A.

A qualified appraisal is not required, but Form 8283, section B, parts I and IV, must be completed for an issue of a security that does not meet the requirements just listed but does meet these requirements:

1. The issue is regularly traded during the computation period in a market for which there is an "interdealer quotation system."

2. The issuer or agent computes the "average trading price" for the same issue for the computation period.

3. The average trading price and total volume of the issue during the computation period are published in a newspaper of general circulation throughout the United States, not later than the last day of the month following the end of the calendar quarter in which the computation period ends.

4. The issuer or agent keeps books and records that list for each transaction during the computation period the date of settlement of the transaction, the name and address of the broker or dealer making the market in which the transaction occurred, and the trading price and volume.

5. The issuer or agent permits the Internal Revenue Service to review the books and records described in item (4) with respect to transactions during the computation period, upon receiving reasonable notice.

An "interdealer quotation system" is any system of general circulation to brokers and dealers that regularly disseminates quotations of obligations by two or more identified brokers or dealers who are not related to either the issuer or agent who computes the average trading price of the security. A quotation sheet prepared and distributed by a broker or dealer in the regular course of business and containing only quotations of that broker or dealer is not an interdealer quotation system.

The average trading price is the average price of all transactions (weighted by volume), other than original issue or redemption transactions, conducted through a US office of a broker or dealer who maintains a market in the issue of the security during the computation period. Bid and asked quotations are not taken into account.

The computation period is weekly during October through December and monthly during January through September. The weekly computation periods during October through December begin with the first Monday in October and end with the first Sunday following the last Monday in December.

NONPUBLICLY TRADED STOCK

If you contribute nonpublicly traded stock for which you claim a deduction of $10,000 or less, a qualified appraisal is not required. However, you must attach Form 8283 to your tax return, with section B, parts I and IV, completed.

Deductions of More Than $500,000 Generally, or $20,000 for Works of Art

If you claim a deduction of more than $500,000 for a donation of property or more than $20,000 for a donation of art, you must attach a qualified appraisal of the property to your tax return. This does not apply to contributions of cash, inventory, publicly traded stock, or intellectual property.

If you do not attach the appraisal, you cannot deduct your contribution, unless your failure to attach the appraisal is due to reasonable cause and not to willful neglect.

CHAPTER 11

Internal Revenue Service Review of Appraisals

IF A TAX RETURN IS AUDITED and a deduction is claimed for a value over $5,000, the Internal Revenue Service, in reviewing an income tax return, may accept the claimed value of the donated property based on information or appraisals sent with the return or may make its own determination of FMV. In either case, the IRS may

- contact the taxpayer to obtain more information,

- refer the valuation problem to an IRS appraiser or valuation specialist,

- refer the issue to the Commissioner's Art Advisory Panel (a group of dealers and museum directors who review and recommend acceptance or adjustment of taxpayers' claimed values for major paintings, sculptures, decorative arts, and antiques), or

- contract with an independent dealer, scholar, or appraiser to appraise the property when the objects require appraisers of highly specialized experience and knowledge.

Responsibility of the Internal Revenue Service

The IRS is responsible for reviewing appraisals, but it is not responsible for making them. Supporting the FMV listed on your return is the donor's responsibility. The IRS does not accept appraisals without question. Nor does the IRS recognize any particular appraiser or organization of appraisers.

Timing of Service Action

The IRS generally does not approve fair market valuations or appraisals before the actual filing of the tax return to which the appraisal applies. In addition, the IRS generally does not issue advance rulings approving or disapproving such appraisals.

Art Valued at $50,000 or More

When donating an item of art that has been appraised at $50,000 or more, a taxpayer may request a "Statement of Value" under Revenue Procedure 96-15 that can be relied on by the donor of the item.

Revenue Procedure 96-15 provides procedures for taxpayers to request a review of art valuations for income, estate, and gift returns. Taxpayers may obtain a Statement of Value from the IRS for an advance review of art valuation claims prior to filing the return. The Statement of Value may then be used to complete the taxpayer's return. The procedure generally applies to an item of art that has been appraised at $50,000 or more. The appraisal submitted must meet specific substantiation requirements. A user fee is charged for each request. Effective February 1, 2020, the current fee for a Statement of Value is $7,500 for one to three items and $400 for each additional item. See Revenue Procedure 2020-01.

Method of Payment for Statement of Value

As modified by Rev. Proc. 2018-01, user fees for Statement of Value requests made pursuant to Rev. Proc. 96-15 must be made by direct debit from a checking or savings account through Pay.gov. Payment confirmations are provided through the Pay.gov portal and should be submitted with the Statement of Value request. Art Appraisal Services will not consider a Statement of Value request complete, and will hold the request in suspense, until the correct user fee is paid through Pay.gov. Use of Pay.gov will replace the mailing or hand delivering of user fees. The use of Pay.gov to submit Statement of Value user fees is mandatory. Information on payment submission can be found at Frequently Asked Questions on Pay.gov. Please refer to the additional instructions on submitting a payment through Pay.gov.

Send requests for a Statement of Value to the address listed below:

Internal Revenue Service/Art Appraisal Services
1111 Constitution Ave., Suite 700
C:AP:SO:ART
Washington, DC 20224-0002
ATTN: AAS

Note: It is recommended that a private delivery service be utilized, as packages sent via USPS are subject to irradiation that may damage professional photographs.

The taxpayer must request the statement before filing the tax return that reports the donation and must also comply with other substantiation and fee requirements. (See IRS Publication 561, p. 4, for summary.)

Penalty for Donors

You may be liable for a penalty if you overstate the value or adjusted basis of donated property.

TWENTY PERCENT PENALTY

The penalty is 20 percent of the underpayment of tax related to the overstatement if

- the value or adjusted basis claimed on the return is 200 percent (150 percent for returns filed after August 17, 2006) or more of the correct amount, and

- you underpaid your tax by more than $5,000 because of the overstatement.

FORTY PERCENT PENALTY

The penalty is 40 percent, rather than 20 percent, if

- the value or adjusted basis claimed on the return is 400 percent (200 percent for returns filed after August 17, 2006) or more of the correct amount, and

- you underpaid your tax by more than $5,000 because of the overstatement.

IRS Form 8283, Noncash Charitable Contributions (Revised 2019)

The purpose of IRS Form 8283 is to report information on noncash charitable contributions. Generally, if the claimed deduction for an item of donated property is more than $5,000, you must attach Form 8283 to your tax return and complete section B.

If you do not attach Form 8283 to your return and complete section B, the deduction will not be allowed unless your failure was due to reasonable cause, and not willful neglect, or was due to a good-faith omission.

If the IRS requests that you submit the form because you did not attach it to your return, you must comply within ninety days of the request or the deduction will be disallowed.

You must attach a separate Form 8283 for each item of contributed property that is not part of a group of similar items. If you contribute similar items of property to the same donee organization, you need attach only one Form 8283 for those items. If you contribute similar items of property to more than one donee organization, you must attach a separate form for each donee.

To receive a tax deduction, Form 8283 must be filed with the donor's tax return for any noncash contributions of $500 or more. This applies to any single item or any group of similar items valued at $500 or more.

For noncash contributions of $500 to $5,000, only section A of Form 8283 needs to be filled out and no qualified appraisal is required.

CHAPTER 12

IRS Form 8283
Noncash Charitable Contributions

FOR NONCASH CONTRIBUTIONS of any single item, or group of similar items, valued at over $5,000, the IRS requires a qualified appraisal by a qualified appraiser, and section B of Form 8283 must be filled out. Side B must be signed by the donor, donee, and the appraiser.

For noncash contributions of art valued at $20,000 or more, a signed copy of the appraisal also must accompany the donor's income tax return.

Form 8283 must be signed and dated by the donor and donee.

Form 8283 must be signed and dated by the appraiser, when an appraisal is required. IRS Form 8283 also requires the appraiser's tax identification number or Social Security number. The tax identification is preferred for security.

Form 8283 requires three signatures and effective date (donor, donee, and appraiser).

Form **8283**
(Rev. November 2019)
Department of the Treasury
Internal Revenue Service

Noncash Charitable Contributions

▶ Attach one or more Forms 8283 to your tax return if you claimed a total deduction
of over $500 for all contributed property.

▶ Go to *www.irs.gov/Form8283* for instructions and the latest information.

OMB No. 1545-0908

Attachment
Sequence No. **155**

Name(s) shown on your income tax return | Identifying number

Note: Figure the amount of your contribution deduction before completing this form. See your tax return instructions.

Section A. Donated Property of $5,000 or Less and Publicly Traded Securities—List in this section **only** an item (or groups of similar items) for which you claimed a deduction of $5,000 or less. Also list publicly traded securities and certain other property even if the deduction is more than $5,000 (see instructions).

| **Part I** | Information on Donated Property—If you need more space, attach a statement. |

1	**(a)** Name and address of the donee organization	**(b)** If donated property is a vehicle (see instructions), check the box. Also enter the vehicle identification number (unless Form 1098-C is attached).	**(c)** Description and condition of donated property (For a vehicle, enter the year, make, model, and mileage. For securities and other property, see instructions.)
A		☐	
B		☐	
C		☐	
D		☐	
E		☐	

Note: If the amount you claimed as a deduction for an item is $500 or less, you do not have to complete columns (e), (f), and (g).

	(d) Date of the contribution	**(e)** Date acquired by donor (mo., yr.)	**(f)** How acquired by donor	**(g)** Donor's cost or adjusted basis	**(h)** Fair market value (see instructions)	**(i)** Method used to determine the fair market value
A						
B						
C						
D						
E						

| **Part II** | Partial Interests and Restricted Use Property—Complete lines 2a through 2e if you gave less than an entire interest in a property listed in Part I. Complete lines 3a through 3c if conditions were placed on a contribution listed in Part I; also attach the required statement (see instructions). |

2a Enter the letter from Part I that identifies the property for which you gave less than an entire interest ▶ _____

If Part II applies to more than one property, attach a separate statement.

b Total amount claimed as a deduction for the property listed in Part I: **(1)** For this tax year ▶ _____

(2) For any prior tax years ▶ _____

c Name and address of each organization to which any such contribution was made in a prior year (complete only if different from the donee organization above):

Name of charitable organization (donee)

Address (number, street, and room or suite no.)

City or town, state, and ZIP code

d For tangible property, enter the place where the property is located or kept ▶ _____

e Name of any person, other than the donee organization, having actual possession of the property ▶ _____

		Yes	No
3a	Is there a restriction, either temporary or permanent, on the donee's right to use or dispose of the donated property?		
b	Did you give to anyone (other than the donee organization or another organization participating with the donee organization in cooperative fundraising) the right to the income from the donated property or to the possession of the property, including the right to vote donated securities, to acquire the property by purchase or otherwise, or to designate the person having such income, possession, or right to acquire?		
c	Is there a restriction limiting the donated property for a particular use?		

For Paperwork Reduction Act Notice, see separate instructions.   Cat. No. 62299J   Form **8283** (Rev. 11-2019)

Figure 12.1. Form 8283 side A

Name(s) shown on your income tax return	Identifying number

Section B. Donated Property Over $5,000 (Except Publicly Traded Securities, Vehicles, Intellectual Property or Inventory Reportable in Section A)—Complete this section for one item (or a group of similar items) for which you claimed a deduction of more than $5,000 per item or group (except contributions reportable in Section A). Provide a separate form for each item donated unless it is part of a group of similar items. A qualified appraisal is generally required for items reportable in Section B. See instructions.

Part I	**Information on Donated Property**

4 Check the box that describes the type of property donated.

a ☐ Art* (contribution of $20,000 or more)	**d** ☐ Art* (contribution of less than $20,000)	**g** ☐ Collectibles**	**j** ☐ Other
b ☐ Qualified Conservation Contribution	**e** ☐ Other Real Estate	**h** ☐ Intellectual Property	
c ☐ Equipment	**f** ☐ Securities	**i** ☐ Vehicles	

*Art includes paintings, sculptures, watercolors, prints, drawings, ceramics, antiques, decorative arts, textiles, carpets, silver, rare manuscripts, historical memorabilia, and other similar objects.

**Collectibles include coins, stamps, books, gems, jewelry, sports memorabilia, dolls, etc., but not art as defined above.

Note: In certain cases, you must attach a qualified appraisal of the property. See instructions.

5	**(a)** Description of donated property (if you need more space, attach a separate statement)	**(b)** If any tangible personal property or real property was donated, give a brief summary of the overall physical condition of the property at the time of the gift	**(c)** Appraised fair market value
A			
B			
C			
D			

	(d) Date acquired by donor (mo., yr.)	**(e)** How acquired by donor	**(f)** Donor's cost or adjusted basis	**(g)** For bargain sales, enter amount received	**(h)** Amount claimed as a deduction	**(i)** Date of contribution
					See instructions	
A						
B						
C						
D						

Part II	**Taxpayer (Donor) Statement**—List each item included in Part I above that the appraisal identifies as having a value of $500 or less. See instructions.

I declare that the following item(s) included in Part I above has to the best of my knowledge and belief an appraised value of not more than $500 (per item). Enter identifying letter from Part I and describe the specific item. See instructions. ▶ _____

Signature of taxpayer (donor) ▶   Date ▶

Part III	**Declaration of Appraiser**

I declare that I am not the donor, the donee, a party to the transaction in which the donor acquired the property, employed by, or related to any of the foregoing persons, or married to any person who is related to any of the foregoing persons. And, if regularly used by the donor, donee, or party to the transaction, I performed the majority of my appraisals during my tax year for other persons.

Also, I declare that I perform appraisals on a regular basis; and that because of my qualifications as described in the appraisal, I am qualified to make appraisals of the type of property being valued. I certify that the appraisal fees were not based on a percentage of the appraised property value. Furthermore, I understand that a false or fraudulent overstatement of the property value as described in the qualified appraisal or this Form 8283 may subject me to the penalty under section 6701(a) (aiding and abetting the understatement of tax liability). I understand that my appraisal will be used in connection with a return or claim for refund. I also understand that, if there is a substantial or gross valuation misstatement of the value of the property claimed on the return or claim for refund that is based on my appraisal, I may be subject to a penalty under section 6695A of the Internal Revenue Code, as well as other applicable penalties. I affirm that I have not been at any time in the three-year period ending on the date of the appraisal barred from presenting evidence or testimony before the Department of the Treasury or the Internal Revenue Service pursuant to 31 U.S.C. 330(c).

Sign Here

Signature ▶	Title ▶	Date ▶

Business address (including room or suite no.)	Identifying number
City or town, state, and ZIP code	

Part IV	**Donee Acknowledgment**—To be completed by the charitable organization.

This charitable organization acknowledges that it is a qualified organization under section 170(c) and that it received the donated property as described in Section B, Part I, above on the following date ▶ _____

Furthermore, this organization affirms that in the event it sells, exchanges, or otherwise disposes of the property described in Section B, Part I (or any portion thereof) within 3 years after the date of receipt, it will file **Form 8282,** Donee Information Return, with the IRS and give the donor a copy of that form. This acknowledgment does not represent agreement with the claimed fair market value.

Does the organization intend to use the property for an unrelated use? . . . . ▶ ☐ Yes   ☐ No

Name of charitable organization (donee)	Employer identification number	
Address (number, street, and room or suite no.)	City or town, state, and ZIP code	
Authorized signature	Title	Date

Form **8283** (Rev. 11-2019)

Figure 12.2.   Form 8283 side B

CHAPTER 13

Appraisals and Appraisers

IRS Definition of a Qualified Appraisal

A qualified appraisal means an appraisal that is conducted by a qualified appraiser in accordance with generally accepted appraisal standards. It also must meet the relevant requirements of Reg. §l.170A-13c (3) and Notice 2006-96, 2006-46 I.R.B. 902 (available at www.irs.gov/irb/2006-46_IRB/ar13.html) and the IRS Definition of Qualified Appraisal (Notice 2006-96 link (a) (2): § 1.170 A-17 as follows and revised effective January 1, 2019:

- An appraisal conducted, prepared, signed, and dated by a qualified appraiser in accordance with generally accepted appraisal standards.

- Generally accepted appraisal standards are those that are consistent with the substance and principles of the Uniform Standards of Professional Appraisal Practice, or USPAP, as developed by the Appraisal Standards Board of the Appraisal Foundation.

- An appraisal made not earlier than sixty days prior to the contribution and no later than due date (including extensions) of the donor's tax return.

- An appraisal does not involve a prohibited type of appraisal fee.

A qualified appraisal must include all of the following information:
1. a description of the property in sufficient detail for a person who is not generally familiar with the type of property to determine that the property appraised is the property that was (or will be) contributed;

2. the physical condition of any tangible property;

3. the date (or expected date) of contribution;

4. the terms of any agreement or understanding entered into (or expected to be entered into) by or on behalf of the donor that relates to the use, sale, or other disposition of the donated property, such as

   a. temporarily or permanently restricts a donee's right to use or dispose of the donated property,

   b. earmarks the donated property for a particular use, or

   c. reserves to, or confers upon, anyone (other than a donee organization or an organization participating with a donee organization in cooperative fund-raising) any right to the income from the donated property or to the possession of the property, including the right to vote donated securities, to acquire the property by purchase or otherwise, or to designate the person having the income, possession, or right to acquire the property;

5. the name, address, and taxpayer identification number of the qualified appraiser and, if the appraiser is a partner, an employee, or an independent

---

Effective January 1, 2019, the qualified gift appraisal must contain he following declaration by the qualified appraiser:

> I understand that my appraisal will be used in connection with a return or claim for refund. I also understand that, if there is a substantial or gross valuation misstatement of the value of the property claimed on the return or claim for refund that is based on my appraisal, I may be subject to a penalty under section 6695A of the Internal Revenue Code, as well as other applicable penalties.
>
> I affirm that I have not been at any time in the three-year period ending on the date of the appraisal barred from presenting evidence or testimony before the Department of the Treasury or the Internal Revenue Service pursuant to 31 U.S.C. section 330(c).

Moreover, a statement must be included in the qualified gift appraisal stating explicitly that the appraisal was prepared for income tax purposes.

contractor engaged by a person other than the donor, the name, address, and taxpayer identification number of the partnership or the person who employs or engages the qualified appraiser;

6. the qualifications of the qualified appraiser who signs the appraisal, including the appraiser's background, experience, education, and any membership in professional appraisal associations; if the donor uses the appraisal of more than one appraiser, or if two appraisers contribute to the report, each shall comply with the requirements of § 1.170 A-17 and sign the qualified appraisal and the IRS 8283 appraisal summary;

7. a declaration that the appraisal was prepared for income tax purposes;

8. the date or dates on which the property was valued;

9. the appraised fair market value on the date (or expected date) of contribution;

10. the method of valuation used to determine fair market value, such as the income approach, the comparable sales or market data approach, or the replacement cost less depreciation approach; and

11. the specific basis for the valuation, such as any specific comparable sales transaction.

CHAPTER 14
Works of Art and Collectibles

THE FOLLOWING ARE EXAMPLES, as set forth in IRS Publication 561: Determining the Value of Donated Property, of the information that should be included in a description of donated works of art and collections:

1. a complete description of the object, indicating the size, subject matter, medium, name of the artist (or culture), and approximate date created;

2. the cost, date, and manner of acquisition;

3. a history of the item, including proof of authenticity;

4. a professional-quality image of the object; and

5. the facts on which the appraisal was based, such as the following: sales or analysis of similar works by the artist, particularly on or around the valuation date; quoted prices in dealers' catalogs of the artist's works or works of other artists of comparable stature; a record of any exhibitions at which the specific art object had been displayed; the economic state of the art market at the time of valuation, particularly with respect to the specific property; the standing of the artist in his or her profession and in the particular school or time period.

IRS Suggested Individual Object Identification Format for Art Valued over $20,000 and over $50,000

The following is an example of what the IRS has suggested that each appraised object submitted in an individual Object Identification Format for works of fine and decorative art valued over $20,000 and over $50,000. The elements of the Object ID should include:

- effective date of valuation;
- fair market value;
- artist, maker, title, date, or period;
- description of the property;
- medium (materials and techniques);
- dimensions;
- signature, inscriptions, markings, or other identifying details;
- provenance or ownership history;
- exhibition history and literary references;
- condition;
- acquisition date, method, price paid;
- appraisal valuation support;
- auction/gallery and/or private sales of comparable objects;
- reasoning for conclusion of fair market value; and
- a professional-quality image (photograph) of item being appraised.

You must receive the qualified appraisal before the due date, including extensions, of the return on which a charitable contribution deduction is first claimed for the donated property. If the deduction is first claimed on an amended return, the qualified appraisal must be received before the date on which the amended return is filed.

Form 8283, section B, must be attached to your tax return. Generally, you do not need to attach the qualified appraisal itself, but you should keep a copy as long as it may be relevant under the tax law. There are four exceptions:

1. If you claim a deduction of $20,000 or more for donations of art, you must attach a complete copy of the appraisal.

2. If you claim a deduction of more than $500,000 for a donation of property, you must attach a complete copy of the appraisal.

3. If you claim a deduction of more than $500 for an article of clothing, or a household item, that is not in good used condition or better, that you donated after August 17, 2006, you must attach the appraisal.

4. If you claim a deduction in a tax year beginning after August 17, 2006, for an easement or other restriction on the exterior of a building in a historic district, you must attach the appraisal.

Prohibited Appraisal Fee

Generally, no part of the fee arrangement for a qualified appraisal can be based on a percentage of the appraised value of the property. If a fee arrangement is based on what is allowed as a deduction, after Internal Revenue Service examination or otherwise, it is treated as a fee based on a percentage of appraised value. However, appraisals are not disqualified when an otherwise prohibited fee is paid to a generally recognized association that regulates appraisers if

- the association is not organized for profit and no part of its net earnings benefits any private shareholder or individual,

- the appraiser does not receive any compensation from the association or any other persons for making the appraisal, or

- the fee arrangement is not based in whole or in part on the amount of the appraised value that is allowed as a deduction after an IRS examination or otherwise.

Number of Qualified Appraisals

A separate qualified appraisal is required for each item of property that is not included in a group of similar items of property. You need only one qualified appraisal for a group of similar items of property contributed in the same tax year, but you may secure separate appraisals for each item.

A qualified appraisal for a group of similar items must provide all the required information for each item of similar property. The appraiser, however, may provide a group description for selected items the total value of which is not more than $100.

CHAPTER 15
Definition of a Qualified Appraiser and Excluded Individuals

ACCORDING TO THE IRS DEFINITION of Qualified Appraiser (Notice 2006-96 link), and 2018:33 effective January 1, 2019, for purposes of section 170(f)(11) and §1.170A-16(d)(1)(ii) and (e)(1)(ii), a qualified appraiser is an individual who meets all the following requirements:

- The individual has verifiable education and experience and has earned a designation (i.e., accreditation) from a recognized professional appraisal organization for demonstrated competency in valuing the type of property being appraised, or has met certain minimum education and experience requirements:

    1. has successfully completed college or professional-level coursework that is relevant to the property being valued,

    2. has obtained two or more years of experience in valuing the type of property being valued, and

    3. has fully described in the appraisal his or her qualifying education and experience.

- The individual regularly prepares appraisals for which the individual is paid.

- The individual demonstrates verifiable education and experience in valuing the type of property being appraised (i.e., they can make a declaration that they are qualified as either part of the appraisal (appraisal certification) or it can be made as a separate letter or document).

- The individual has not been prohibited from practicing before the Internal Revenue Service at any time during the three-year period ending on the date the appraisal is signed.

- The individual is not an excluded individual (see below).

For real property, the appraiser must be licensed or certified for the type of property being appraised in the state in which the property is located.

In addition, the appraiser must complete IRS Form 8283, section B, part III. More than one appraiser may appraise the property, provided that each complies with the requirements, including signing the qualified appraisal and appraisal summary (IRS Form 8283, section B, part III).

Excluded Individuals

The following persons cannot be qualified appraisers with respect to particular property:

1. The donor of the property or the taxpayer who claims the deduction.

2. The donee of the property.

3. A party to the transaction in which the donor acquired the property being appraised, unless the property is donated within two months of the date of acquisition and its appraised value is not more than its acquisition price. This applies to the person who sold, exchanged, or gave the property to the donor, or any person who acted as an agent for the transferor or donor in the transaction.

4. Any person employed by any of the above persons. For example, if the donor acquired a painting from an art dealer, neither the dealer nor persons employed by the dealer can be qualified appraisers for that painting.

5. Any person related under section 267(b) of the Internal Revenue Code to any of the above persons or married to a person related under section 267(b) to any of the above persons.

6. An appraiser who appraises regularly for a person in (1), (2), or (3) and who does not perform a majority of his or her appraisals made during his or her tax year for other persons.

In addition, a person is not a qualified appraiser for a particular donation if the donor had knowledge of facts that would cause a reasonable person to expect the appraiser to falsely overstate the value of the donated property.

For example, if the donor and the appraiser make an agreement concerning the amount at which the property will be valued, and the donor knows that amount is more than the FMV of the property, the appraiser is not a qualified appraiser for the donation.

Appraisers' Responsibilities: Uniform Standards of Professional Appraisal Practice

The Uniform Standards of Professional Appraisal Practice (USPAP) is the generally recognized ethical and performance standards for the appraisal profession in the United States. USPAP was adopted by the United States Congress in 1989 and contains standards for all types of appraisal services, including real estate, personal property, business, and mass appraisal. Compliance is required for state-licensed and state-certified appraisers involved in federally related real estate transactions. USPAP is updated every two years so that appraisers have the information they need to deliver unbiased and thoughtful opinions of value. The 2020–2021 edition of USPAP will be in effect as of January 1, 2020 and remains in effect until December 31, 2021.

An appraiser must prepare written records of appraisals and retain such records, and the appraisal report, for a period of at least five years after preparation or at least two years after final disposition of any judicial proceeding in which testimony was given, whichever period expires last.

Appraisal Organizations

There are three appraisal organizations that teach, test, and accredit appraisers:

- American Society of Appraisers, www.appraisers.org

- American Association of Appraisers, www.appraisersassoc.org

- International Society of Appraisers, www.isa-appraisers.org

Note well: The American Society of Appraisers' Legal Counsel has summarized the relevant comments and sections from the IRS Final Rule on Noncash Charitable Contribution Substantiation and Appraisal Requirement at www.appraisers.org.

Part Four
Gift Considerations and Perspectives

CHAPTER 16
Bargain Sales

COMPILED AND EDITED BY LAURETTE E. MCCARTHY

A BARGAIN SALE OF PROPERTY to a qualified organization (a sale or exchange for less than the property's fair market value) is partly a charitable contribution and partly a sale or exchange. (Note: Bargain sales for which the gift portions are valued at over $5,000 need to be reported on section B of IRS Form 8283.) Bargain sales require an independent appraisal in order to estimate the fair market value on IRS Form 8283. Often the museum also conducts an internal appraisal, independent of the donor, for its records.

Part That Is a Sale or Exchange

The part of the bargain sale that is a sale or exchange may result in a taxable gain. For more information on determining the amount of any taxable gain, see "Bargain Sales to Charity" in chapter 1 of IRS Publication 544.

Part That Is a Charitable Contribution

Figure the amount of your charitable contribution in three steps:

Step 1. Subtract the amount you received for the property from the property's fair market value at the time of sale. This gives you the fair market value of the contributed part.

Step 2. Find the adjusted basis of the contributed part. It equals FMV of the contributed part divided by the FMV of the entire property.

Step 3. Determine whether the amount of your charitable contribution is the fair market value of the contributed part (which you found in step 1) or the adjusted basis of the contributed part (which you found in step 2). Generally, if the property sold was capital gain property, your charitable contribution is the fair market value of the contributed part. If it was ordinary income property, your charitable contribution is the adjusted basis of the contributed part. See the ordinary income property and capital gain property rules (discussed earlier) for more information.

EXAMPLE

You sell ordinary income property with a fair market value of $10,000 to a church for $2,000. Your basis is $4,000, and your adjusted gross income is $20,000. You make no other contributions during the year. The fair market value of the contributed part of the property is $8,000 ($10,000 – $2,000). The adjusted basis of the contributed part is $3,200, which equals $4,000 × ($8,000 divided by $10,000).

Because the property is ordinary income property, your charitable contribution deduction is limited to the adjusted basis of the contributed part. You can deduct $3,200.

SAMPLE BARGAIN SALE ACKNOWLEDGMENT LETTER (Also refer to side B of IRS Form 8283.)

Dear Donor/Vendor:

On behalf of the Board of Trustees [or other applicable body or officer] of [institution name], I wish to thank you for the gift inherent in your recent bargain sale to the museum of [object description] for the purchase price of $ [price]. This gift was made on [official date of gift, typically the date payment was made].

We would like to acknowledge your gift with the following credit line. Please confirm that this credit line will be acceptable to you:

Museum Purchase and a Gift from [Donor Name]

Please be aware that if the difference in the fair market value and the reduced price (amount of the gift) is more than $5,000, you will need to file an IRS Form 8283 and seek a qualified appraisal of the [object] if you wish to claim a tax deduction for the gift portion of this sale. If you have any questions, please seek advice from your tax accountant.

Please note that no goods or services were provided in exchange for this gift. This letter is necessary to qualify you for any charitable tax deduction on your contribution. Please retain it for your records.

Once again, on behalf of [institution], I thank you for your generous contribution.

Sincerely,
[Officer]

CHAPTER 17
Promised Gifts and Bequests

COMPILED AND EDITED BY LAURETTE E. MCCARTHY

PROMISED GIFTS AND BEQUESTS allow a donor to commit to and make a donation in his or her lifetime or upon his or her death. Promised (testamentary) gifts may be made by the donor in a letter expressing the donor's intent to give a specific object to the museum at a future date. Museums often have a draft letter as a guide for donors, or the donors can initiate a promised gift with their letter before actually signing a legal binding agreement. Often a museum may suggest that the donor include the gift to the museum in his or her will to ensure that the donor's promised gift will be completed. A promised gift left at a museum should be considered an incoming loan because a promised gift does not transfer title without official and legally binding documents.

SAMPLE PARTIAL INTEREST GIFT AGREEMENT
PARTIAL INTEREST GIFT AGREEMENT

[Donor Names, Donor Addresses]

Hereby jointly, and each of us individually, irrevocably gives, assigns, and transfers to [institution's name, city, state], (hereinafter "the Museum") an undivided X% right, title, and interest, together with an equal percentage of copyright and associated interest which we may have, in the following object as an absolute and unrestricted gift:

[Description of object]

Furthermore, we, the Donors, hereby confirm our pledge to give an additional undivided X% right, title, and interest in the Gift in the years 20XX, 20XX, etc., it being our intention that our remaining and final interest in this Gift shall pass to the Museum by the year 20XX, and that at that time, the Museum shall become the sole owner of the Gift.

This pledge is irrevocable and shall extend to and be binding upon the executor, administrator, trustee, heirs, and assigns of the survivor of us, the Donors. Should this Gift not be completed prior to the death of the survivor, the failure to include a specific bequest of the Gift to the Museum in the survivor's Will or Trust shall not release the executor or administrator of such Will or trustee of such Trust from the obligation of delivering the Gift to the Museum in accordance herewith.

We, the Donors, acknowledge that we have been advised that the Museum must take "substantial possession" of this Gift between now and when the final interest in the Gift passes to the Museum. Until completion of the Gift, the Museum agrees to provide insurance coverage under its Fine Arts Insurance Policy in an amount sufficient to protect the Donors and the Museum against physical loss or damage to the Gift. The Donors shall provide the Museum with an initial insurance value and any subsequent revisions to that value. In the event of a loss, the Donors shall be limited to compensation equivalent to the value of their percentage of ownership in the Gift at the time of the loss.

The Donors hereby grant the Museum unrestricted and exclusive rights to photograph, telecast, or reproduce the Gift for educational, catalogue, and publicity purposes. Where possible, the Donors shall be credited as stated on the credit line below.

Until completion of the donation, we, the Donors, wish that the Gift be identified to the public and in the records of the Museum as:

Partial and Promised Gift of _____

After completion of the donation, we wish that the Gift be identified to the public and in the records of the Museum as:

Gift of _____

To the best of the Donors' knowledge and belief, this gift is free and clear of all encumbrances and restrictions and since [date] has not been imported or exported into or from any country contrary to its laws.

This agreement is unconditional and remains fully effective regardless of the changes in value or attribution respecting the Gift. This agreement shall be governed by the laws of the state of [name of the state].

Signature of Donor _____ Date _____

Signature of Donor _____ Date _____

I certify that this pledge agreement was accepted by the proper authority of [institution's name], and that it correctly states the agreement between us.

Dated this _____ day of _____, 20_____

[institution's name]

By: _____

The Donors acknowledge that they have not received any tax advice from [institution's name] in connection with this donation and have relied on their own tax and financial advisers concerning the donation.

The Donors have received no goods or services in consideration of this gift.

Please sign both copies of the Partial Interest Gift Agreement and return them to [institution's name] in the enclosed envelope. A countersigned copy will be returned to you and will serve as the formal acknowledgment of your partial and promised gift.

CHAPTER 18

Fractional Gifts/Partial Interest Gifts

COMPILED AND EDITED BY LAURETTE E. MCCARTHY

FRACTIONAL GIFTS ARE GIFTS made for tax purposes. A fractional interest in tangible personal property is an undivided portion of your entire interest in the property.

A donor may continue to give a museum partial ownership in a work of art; however, now the remainder ownership must be completed within ten years or the donor's death, whichever occurs first.

You cannot deduct a charitable contribution of a fractional interest in tangible personal property unless all interests in the property are held immediately before the contribution by you, the donor, or you and the qualifying organization receiving the contribution.

If you make an additional contribution later, the fair market value of that contribution is the smaller of

- the fair market value of the property at the time of the initial fractional contribution, or

- the fair market value of the property at the time of the additional contribution.

After the Pension Protection Act of 2006

The Pension Protection Act created new limitations on the donation of fractional interests after August 17, 2006. These limitations are now memorialized in IRS Publication 526.

Once a fractional gift is made, the value of any subsequent gifts is now limited to the lesser of the initial fair market value of the contribution or the later fair market value of the contribution. In other words, if the value of the item goes down, the fair market value deduction goes down, but if the value of the item goes up, the deduction does not go up. The donor is entitled only to the same value as the initial fractional interest contribution.

The gift must be completed within the earlier of ten years or the death of the taxpayer. This means that the donation of all fractions owned by the donor must be completed and donated within ten years.

The donee institution must take substantial physical possession or make use of the property during the period of the gift. If any of these conditions is not met, then the deduction previously taken by the taxpayer will be recaptured, with interest at 10 percent.

For additional information, please consult "AAMD Tax Primer" by Anita N. Difanis and Andy Finch, Association of Art Museum Directors Washington, DC. AAMD issued their tax primer in 2014 that is available for download on their website at: https://aamd.org/advocacy/key-issues/tax-matters.

CHAPTER 19

Restricted and Unrestricted Gifts

COMPILED AND EDITED BY LAURETTE E. MCCARTHY

AN OUTRIGHT GIFT, one that is unrestricted, is the standard and best practice for museums and donors. If, however, a donor wishes to place a specific restriction on the gift—for example, that the work must be exhibited or cannot be sold—this request should be made at the time the gift is offered. This allows the museum staff to determine if such restrictions can be honored prior to accepting the gift.

CHAPTER 20

Cultural Patrimony and Ethnographic Gifts

ELIZABETH MORTON

Complying with NAGPRA

NAGPRA, the Native American Graves Protection and Repatriation Act (1990), covers artwork and other cultural patrimony as well as human remains, sacred objects, and funerary objects created by or belonging to Native American and Native Hawaiian tribes or the descendants of those groups. Most museums are required by law to return any such item in their collection for which there is a legitimate claim of ownership.

Following are relevant excerpts from "Complying with NAGPRA" by C. Timothy McKeown, Amanda Murphy, and Jennifer Schansberg, from *Museum Registration Methods*, 5th edition.

> NAGPRA was enacted on November 16, 1990, to formally affirm the rights of lineal descendants, Indian tribes, and Native Hawaiian organizations to custody of Native American human remains, funerary objects, sacred objects, and objects of cultural patrimony that are in the control of federal agencies and museums. The law made it a federal offense to sell, purchase, or use profits from Native American human remains, funerary objects, sacred objects, and objects of cultural patrimony in certain situations. Private individuals and museums that do not receive federal funds and are not part of a larger entity that receives federal funds are not required to comply with the act.

In summary,

- human remains, funerary objects, and sacred objects may be claimed by lineal descendants, Indian tribes, and Native Hawaiian organizations;

- objects of cultural patrimony may only be claimed by Indian tribes and Native Hawaiian organizations; and

- nonfederally recognized Indian groups do not have standing to make a direct claim under the statute.

Compliance with NAGPRA

There are eight specific ways that a museum might fail to comply with NAGPRA:

1. Sell or transfer any human remains, funerary object, sacred object, or object of cultural patrimony without complying with the statute.

2. Fail to complete a summary of collections that may include unassociated funerary objects, sacred objects, or objects of cultural patrimony.

3. Fail to complete an inventory of human remains or associated funerary objects.

4. Fail to notify culturally affiliated Indian tribes or Native Hawaiian organizations within six months after completion of the inventory.

5. Refuse to repatriate human remains, funerary objects, sacred objects, or objects of cultural patrimony to a lineal descendant or culturally affiliated Indian tribe or Native Hawaiian organization.

6. Repatriate human remains, funerary objects, sacred objects, or objects of cultural patrimony prior to publishing a notice in the Federal Register.

7. Fail to consult with lineal descendants or affiliated Indian tribes or Native Hawaiian organizations.

8. Fail to inform recipients that items have been treated with pesticides.[1]

For current information regarding NAGPRA, including laws and regulations, databases, and notices, see the U.S. Department of the Interior National Park Service NAGPRA website: www.nps.gov/nagpra.

COMPLYING WITH NATIONAL AND INTERNATIONAL LAW WHEN DONATING CULTURAL PROPERTY ORIGINATING FROM OTHER NATIONS

The past several years have witnessed a growing number of international claims on objects from collectors and museums in Europe and the United States by cultural groups and nations around the world. It is imperative to be up to date with databases on objects as well as laws governing their transfer of ownership. This section will cover objects that are already in the United States, and while many laws and regulations overlap, the importation of objects has some additional requirements covered in the section "Importation Restrictions and Documentation" below.

In 1970, the United Nations Educational, Scientific and Cultural Organization (UNESCO) created the Convention on the Means of Prohibiting and Preventing the Illicit Import, Export, and Transfer of Ownership of Cultural Property. This is often referred to as the UNESCO World Heritage Convention or Act. The United States accepted the convention in 1983, establishing the Convention on Cultural Property Implementation Act, H.R. 4566 (CCPIA or CPIA). In 2004, under the direction of Congress, the State Department created the Cultural Antiquities Force, which uses six federal agencies to combat trafficking in antiquities in the United States.

Recently, in 2015–2016, the United States reaffirmed its support of the convention by adding additional regulations through the Protect and Preserve International Cultural Property Act, H.R. 1493, and creating the Cultural Heritage Coordinating Committee under the Department of State to bring agencies and organizations together to enforce laws and coordinate information.

Objects that are covered under the UNESCO World Heritage Convention must come from member states and are defined as follows in Article 1:

> For the purposes of this Convention, the term "cultural property"
> means property which, on religious or secular grounds, is specifically

designated by each State as being of importance for archaeology, prehistory, history, literature, art or science and which belongs to the following categories:

a. Rare collections and specimens of fauna, flora, minerals and anatomy, and objects of paleontological interest;

b. property relating to history, including the history of science and technology and military and social history, to the life of national leaders, thinkers, scientists and artists, and to events of national importance;

c. products of archaeological excavations (including regular and clandestine) or of archaeological discoveries;

d. elements of artistic or historical monuments or archaeological sites which have been dismembered;

e. antiquities more than one hundred years old, such as inscriptions, coins and engraved seals;

f. objects of ethnological interest;

g. property of artistic interest, such as:

   i. pictures, paintings and drawings produced entirely by hand on any support and in any material (excluding industrial designs and manufactured articles decorated by hand);

   ii. original works of statuary art and sculpture in any material;

   iii. original engravings, prints and lithographs;

   iv. original artistic assemblages and montages in any material;

h. rare manuscripts and incunabula, old books, documents and publications of special interest (historical, artistic, scientific, literary, etc.) singly or in collections;

i. postage, revenue and similar stamps, singly or in collections;

j. archives, including sound, photographic and cinematographic archives;

k. articles of furniture more than one hundred years old and old musical instruments.

Any objects that entered the United States after 1983 are subject to law, but many museums will honor the original UNESCO Convention date of 1970. This means that donors may be asked to produce import certificates and/or other records of provenance when giving these types of objects.

In addition to legal conventions, there are a number of state and cultural groups making international claims on certain objects that were stolen, questionably acquired, or taken by force before 1970. The history of these objects, such as the Parthenon sculptures from Greece, is well documented and has often involved extensive legal proceedings. For example, since 1960, the Edo Kingdom of Nigeria has been seeking restitution for royal bronze and ivory sculptures from Benin City, which the British military took by force in 1897. While the focus has been on the restitution of works from British and German museums, many of these royal objects from Benin are scattered in museums and collections in the United States. US museums have been paying special attention to the case, and some may decide to return objects to Nigeria, even though they were taken out of Nigeria long before 1970.

The following websites are particularly useful in researching current regulations:

- For the UNESCO World Heritage Act or Convention, with lists of member states and links to databases listing stolen and endangered objects, see www.unesco.org/new/en/culture/themes/illicit-trafficking-of-cultural-property/1970-convention.

- For US regulations and information on tasks forces and committees, see the US Department of State Bureau of Educational and Cultural Affairs Cultural Heritage Center website at www.unesco.org/new/en/culture/themes/illicit-trafficking-of-cultural-property/1970-convention.

Importation Restrictions and Documentation

Museums should ensure that gifts created and originating from outside the United States have been imported legally. International and US donors should understand that museums will require them to attest to and provide documentation regarding the legal importation of the donated material.

Following are some issues for both the donor and the museum to consider regarding importation and gifts:

- Work with a licensed customs broker when importing a gift for consideration or acceptance to ensure compliance with US import regulations and proper documentation.

- Ensure that the objects or rare species have been exported legally from their country of origin.

- Exercise due diligence with respect to provenance research regarding Nazi-era material, culturally sensitive objects, and any property that could conceivably have been stolen at a point in its history. Museums in the United States actively contribute to a national database, Nazi-Era Provenance Internet Portal (nepip.org), by listing any objects in their collections that changed hands between 1933 and 1945 in Continental Europe.

- Document compliance and research.

The section "Complying with National and International Law When Donating Cultural Property Originating from Other Nations" briefly describes the international regulations that define and apply to protected cultural heritage. A licensed customs broker will be responsible for proper documentation and will ensure that the relevant laws have been followed. However, there are additional resources for collectors and donors who wish to import cultural property. The United States has active bilateral cultural property agreements with over twenty nations, which can be found on the website https://eca.state.gov/cultural-heritage-center/cultural-property-advisory-committee/current-import-restrictions.

This list changes, especially with emergency import restrictions, which can be made by the Department of State based on recommendations by the Cultural Property Advisory Committee, pursuant to 19 U.S.C. 2603. These are often put in place in regions affected by war or where there are recent archaeological discoveries.

Donors should also understand that they must have possession of the objects for at least one year prior to the donation in order to qualify for a full tax deduction.

Racine Berkow covers relevant information in the chapter "Import and Export" from *Museum Registration Methods*, 5th edition.

Following are a few excerpts:

Import

In general, works valued at more than [$2500] require a formal entry filed with U.S. Customs. An individual or corporation may clear its own shipment; however, this clearance is a time-consuming and sometimes complicated process, depending on what commodity is being imported. In order to facilitate the process, one often hires a customs broker.

Qualifications for Agents

Import-Licensed Broker. The brokerage company should be licensed by U.S. Customs. To obtain this license, the company has been investigated and meets the fiscal, organizational, and security requirements as described in the "Customs Regulations of the United States of America." A licensed individual who has passed an examination and whose background has been investigated must be responsible for running the day-to-day operations of the company. The company must have a valid permit to operate in a particular port of entry or can be approved to file entry in any port in the U.S. The company must also be bonded.

Many companies perform import services in conjunction with a licensed broker. However, by law, the importer must be allowed to have contact with the broker directly.

Working with a licensed company guarantees that one is working with a corporation that meets very stringent legal standards. In order to maintain its permit, the company must continue to comply with the most recent customs regulations. Should the company not perform in an acceptable manner, the client has the right to redress under specific procedures within US law.[2]

Notes

1. Timothy McKeown, Amanda Murphy, and Jennifer Schansberg, "Complying with NAGPRA," *Museum Registration Methods*, 5th edition (Washington, DC: AAM Press, 2010), pp. 448–52.

2. Racine Berkow, "Import and Export," *Museum Registration Methods*, 5th edition (Washington, DC: AAM Press, 2010), pp. 338–41.

CHAPTER 21

Cultural Patrimony Chart

ELIZABETH MORTON

Types of Objects	Conventions and Laws That Apply	Key Responsibilities of the Donor	Website Resources
Cultural Property Created by or Belonging to Native Americans and Native Hawaiian Tribes Artwork and other cultural patrimony, as well as human remains, sacred objects, and funerary objects, created by or belonging to Native American and Native Hawaiian tribes or the descendants of those groups	The 1990 Native American Graves Protection and Repatriation Act (NAGPRA)	Do not violate the regulations of NAGPRA when acquiring, selling, or donating works. Keep sales and collection documents and all other records of provenance history of objects. Understand that under NAGPRA you may be required to repatriate an object to lineal descendants, Indian tribes, or Native Hawaiian organizations.	For current information regarding NAGPRA, including laws and regulations, databases, and notices, see the US Department of the Interior National Park Service NAGPRA website: www.nps.gov/nagpra.
Cultural Property Originating from Other Nations Property that, on religious or secular grounds, is specifically designated by UNESCO Convention member states as being of importance for archaeology, prehistory, history, literature, art, or science and that belongs to categories defined in article 1 of the Convention.	The 1970 UNESCO Convention on the Means of Prohibiting and Preventing the Illicit Import, Export, and Transfer of Ownership of Cultural Property (UNESCO World Heritage Convention), accepted in 1983 by the United States Convention on Cultural Property Implementation Act, H.R. 4566 (CCPIA or CPIA), or the 2016 Protect and Preserve International Cultural Property Act, H.R. 1493	Do not violate the regulations of the 1970 UNESCO World Heritage Convention, CPIA, or the United States Convention on Cultural Property Implementation Act when acquiring, selling, or donating works. Keep sales and collection documents and all other records of provenance history of objects. For any objects imported after 1983, provide required customs documents and import certificates. Understand that some museums will abide by the 1970 UNESCO convention date and may take into consideration earlier historic claims on specific objects.	For the UNESCO World Heritage Act or Convention, with lists of member states and links to databases listing stolen and endangered objects, see www.unesco.org/new/en/culture/themes/illicit-trafficking-of-cultural-property/1970-convention. For US regulations and information on task forces and committees, see the US Department of State Bureau of Educational and Cultural Affairs Cultural Heritage Center website: www.unesco.org/new/en/culture/themes/illicit-trafficking-of-cultural-property/1970-convention.

Imported Cultural Property			
Property that, on religious or secular grounds, is specifically designated by UNESCO Convention member states as being of importance for archaeology, prehistory, history, literature, art, or science and that belongs to categories defined in article 1 of the Convention.	The UNESCO World Heritage Convention, accepted in 1983 by the United States Convention on Cultural Property Implementation Act, H.R. 4566 (CCPIA or CPIA), or the 2016 Protect and Preserve International Cultural Property Act, H.R. 1493	Do not violate the regulations of the 1970 UNESCO World Heritage Convention, CPIA, or the United States Convention on Cultural Property Implementation Act. File a formal entry with US Customs for anything valued at more than $2,500. Work with a licensed customs broker when importing a gift for consideration or acceptance to ensure compliance with US import regulations and proper documentation.	For the UNESCO World Heritage Act or Convention, with lists of member states and links to databases listing stolen and endangered objects, see www.unesco.org/new/en/culture/themes/illicit-trafficking-of-cultural-property/1970-convention

For US regulations and information on task forces and committees, see the US Department of State Bureau of Educational and Cultural Affairs Cultural Heritage Center website: www.unesco.org/new/en/culture/themes/illicit-trafficking-of-cultural-property/1970-convention

The United States has active bilateral cultural property agreements with over twenty nations, which can be found on the website https://eca.state.gov/cultural-heritage-center/cultural-property-advisory-committee/current-import-restrictions |

Part Five

Ownership Perspectives and Fair Market Value

CHAPTER 22

Conveyance of Intellectual Rights and Copyright Chart

CHRISTINE STEINER

A COPYRIGHT IS A FORM OF PROTECTION provided by a national government to creators of original works of authorship, including literary and artistic objects and certain other intellectual works. For additional information, please consult Christine Steiner (ed.), *A Museum Guide to Copyright and Trademark* (Washington, DC: AAM Press, 1999; available at www.aam-us.org).

Copyright Term	Pre-1999	New
Subsisting (pre-1978) copyrights	28 years, + 47-year renewal term = 75 years	28 years, + 67-year renewal term = 95 years
Works created on or after January 1, 1978	Life of the author plus 50 years	Life of the author plus 70 years
Joint works	Same as above, measured from life of last surviving author	Same as above, measured from life of last surviving author
Anonymous and pseudonymous works and works made for hire	75 years from publication or 100 years from creation, whichever expires first	95 years from publication or 120 years from creation, whichever expires first

Copyright Term	Pre-1999	New
Works created but not published before 1978	Same as post–January 1978 works, but term expires no earlier than December 31, 2002 If work is published before December 31, 2002, term shall not expire until December 31, 2027	Same as post–January 1978. works, but term expires no earlier than December 31, 2002 (no change from previous law) If work is published before December 31, 2002, term shall not expire until December 31, 2047
Presumption as to author's death	After 75 years from publication or 100 years from creation, whichever expires first; the author is presumed to have been dead for 50 years if Copyright Office records do not indicate that the author is still living or died within the past 50 years	After 95 years from publication or 120 years from creation, whichever expires first; the author is presumed to have been dead for 70 years if Copyright Office records do not indicate that the author is still living or died within the past 70 years
Termination	Pre-1978 grants may be terminated during 5-year period commencing 56 years from date copyright was first secured	If previous termination right has already expired and was not exercised, copyright owner has a new termination right during 5-year period commencing 75 years from date copyright was first secured

Source: David Carson, General Counsel, US Copyright Office.

For a more thorough discussion, see Christine Steiner, "Copyright" in Museum Registration Methods, *eds. Rebecca Buck and Jean A. Gilmore, 5th ed. (Washington, DC: AAM Press, 2010), 427–35. Also, for the most recent discussion, please consult the chapter "Copyright" by Melissa Levine and Christine Steiner in John E. Simmons and Toni Kiser,* Museum Registration Methods, *6th edition, Rowman & Littlefield, New York and the American Alliance of Museums, 2020, pp. 465–75.*

CHAPTER 23

Artists' and Artists Foundations' Gifts to Museums

SHARON S. THEOBALD

SINCE THE 1970S, an artist may not claim the fair market value (FMV) of self-created works donated by the maker to a qualifying nonprofit organization. The artist may only claim the cost of materials used in creating the works. The law says that the deduction is limited to the cost of the materials. This law applies to family members' donations (spouses and children) as well as trades with other artists (each donate the other's artwork). Unless you have paid for the art at a legitimate price, you cannot take the deduction for more than the cost of materials. Donation of other intellectual property, such as patents, may be allowed as a deduction, but the donor must verify whether the property is allowed and what documentation will be required when claiming the deduction.

If a spouse, child, or fellow artist buys the painting from the artist and then donates it, the FMV deduction could/would apply, as long as there is proof of the sale: money transfers, cancelled checks, or other paper trails. Basically, a purchase has to take place for the full FMV deduction to apply. If the widow/widower inherits and then donates a painting, the full FMV deduction could/would apply.

Artists themselves can donate to museums, and it is standard practice to note that the artist maintains the copyright to the work of art. The assignment of the copyright rests with the artist/maker; it is not assigned to the museum as part of the gift. When living artists and creators donate contemporary or unique works to a museum, the Deed of Gift can include a section for the artist to outline the material and techniques required for future conservation needs or collection storage considerations.

CHAPTER 24

Copyright Does Not Transfer with the Gift

LUKE NIKAS AND MAAREN A. SHAH

FINE ART IS EXPENSIVE TO ACQUIRE. The best works are in limited supply. Some artists' works rarely come on the market. You are therefore excited by the news you have just received: a generous artist, foundation, or collector offers to donate a significant collection to your museum. Everything seems in order: the works are authentic; the provenance is clean; the gift supports the museum's mission; and the museum has grand plans to research, exhibit, publish, and promote the art. There are internal discussions about potential exhibitions, hiring an editor to prepare a special publication or catalogue raisonné, contracting vendors to create products for the gift shop that depict the works, and expanding the museum's programming and website to provide increased public access to the art. These projects will be time-consuming and expensive for the museum, but the expected contribution to scholarship, reputational gains, and earned income potential will be worth the investment.

These plans have a key theme in common: the museum intends to publish images of the donated artworks, which requires intellectual property licenses or an exception under the governing laws. Therein lies the complexity. It might seem counterintuitive, but the copyright in the work that's being offered to you does not follow the work. Copyrights reside in the image that the artist created, not the physical artwork itself. The artist is the "author" of the image, and the artist usually owns the copyright unless it has been transferred by agreement or bequest. And so, transferring an artwork to a museum does not transfer any rights to publish an image of the artwork—not on products, not on the website, not in any other form unless a license is obtained or an exception under the copyright laws applies.

Museums that accept significant gifts must therefore understand the contours of these exceptions and, if none applies, the licenses they must obtain before executing their plans. Failing to do so could materially impact the museum's ability to use images of the artworks in exhibition catalogs and promotional materials or on the museum's public website. It could affect the museum's ability to create a catalogue raisonné of the relevant artist's works. The end result could be devastating: prohibiting the museum from carrying out its plans for the gift and eliminating the benefits that made the gift so attractive. This is not abstract discourse about legal theories and possible problems. Indeed, the legal case unfolding over Robert Indiana's estate illustrates these issues and highlights diligence the museum should undertake.

A Case Study: Robert Indiana

Robert Indiana was a famous American artist. His iconic *LOVE* image is one of the most recognized artworks in the world: it graced a US postage stamp in 1973, and *LOVE* sculptures have been displayed in museums and public spaces around the world. It is also among the most frequently infringed images. Over time, Indiana's iconic artwork has been commercialized through its unauthorized appearance on cheap "knock-offs" like keychains, T-shirts, and posters. The rampant illegal reproductions of *LOVE*, without the artist's consent, damaged Indiana's brand and the value of his artwork.

To protect his artistic legacy and the intellectual property in his artwork, and as a counterweight to the unlicensed goods cluttering the market, in the mid-1990s, Indiana empowered Morgan Art Foundation to protect and enforce his intellectual property in several images, including *LOVE*. Indiana conveyed to Morgan Art Foundation all "copyright, trademark, and other rights" in these images and granted Morgan Art Foundation the exclusive right to reproduce, promote, and sell these images throughout the world. Morgan Art Foundation also had the right to sue for any infringement of the rights Indiana conveyed. Later, Indiana authorized an adviser to Morgan Art Foundation to prepare the catalogue raisonné of his complete oeuvre. Morgan Art Foundation began to enforce these copyrights. The illegal reproductions of Indiana's art subsided but did not disappear.

In 2018, Morgan Art Foundation filed a lawsuit in the US District Court for the Southern District of New York against individuals alleged to have forged artworks that were falsely attributed to Indiana and contained some of Indiana's most famous images.[1] This lawsuit, filed one day before Indiana died, intended to protect Indiana's legacy and art by enforcing the intellectual property rights against alleged forgers. The lawsuit included contractual claims against Indiana himself stemming from his agreement to transfer the intellectual property rights to Morgan Art Foundation as well as Indiana's written agreement to cooperate with Morgan Art Foundation whenever it sought to enforce those rights.[2]

Following Indiana's death, however, his estate sought to terminate Morgan Art Foundation's rights.[3] It also sought to interfere with the publication of the Robert Indiana catalogue raisonné and the website depicting Indiana's art.[4] In response, Morgan Art Foundation alleged that it had invested millions of dollars and over two decades of work promoting Indiana's legacy on the basis of its contractual agreements with Indiana. It also owned a significant collection of Indiana's artworks. The catalogue raisonné was well under way, and the website about Indiana had been live for years. Notwithstanding years of effort to promote and secure Indiana's legacy, Morgan Art Foundation's intellectual property rights came under siege. As of the date of this publication, that litigation is still pending in the Manhattan federal court.

This dispute highlights two cautionary notes.

First, the same attacks launched against Morgan Art Foundation for its use of Indiana's images could be launched against a museum seeking to publish images of artworks. Publishing images on a museum website, publishing a catalogue raisonné, and otherwise using the images can trigger litigation by the rights holder or someone who believes it should be the rights holder.

Second, the risk of litigation exists primarily because of the disconnect between the ownership of art and the ownership of copyrights in the images. Specifically, ownership of a physical work of art is distinct from ownership of the copyright: they are an entirely separate bundle of rights. For that reason, the museum will not obtain legal rights to use the intellectual property simply by receiving a gift of the art containing the protected image.[5] It is the rights holder, not the owner of the physical work in question, who has the right to permit others to create works derived from the original. 17 U.S. Code § 106(2). The ability to transfer intellectual property rights can make careful planning even more difficult. For example, Indiana contractually transferred his intellectual property rights to Morgan Art Foundation, in perpetuity. Morgan Art Foundation has therefore controlled the intellectual property rights for decades. Yet the estate, claiming a right of return even though the original grant was made "in perpetuity," sought to take back those rights after Indiana died. Parties seeking permissions to use the images created by Indiana are left with uncertainty.

These complexities raise important questions that must be answered, as completely as possible, before accepting a gift. How does the museum considering a gift of art sort out a dispute over the rights? How does it find certainty about the types of projects it will be permitted to undertake? These questions apply to the works of every artist, because the risk of disputes exists until the museum obtains the right to use the images—or, at least, accurate advice that a safe harbor applies. The museum must consult legal experts for guidance if it is uncertain about its legal rights. Accepting the gift without careful planning could spell disaster.

Navigating Copyright Issues in Connection with Gifts to Museums

To navigate the intellectual property issues that could arise from a proposed gift, the museum must start at the beginning: How does it intend to use images of the artworks? For example, will it redesign its website to highlight the works? Will it hire an editor to prepare a catalogue raisonné, given that the museum will now own a significant number of an artist's works—or a highly significant work by the artist? What about programming? Will it create exhibition catalogs, books, or other materials? Does it intend to contract with vendors to have products created for the gift shop? Without careful planning, these and any other publications of imagery from the artworks are fair game for legal challenges.

Once the museum determines its plan for using the images, it must identify who owns the rights. This is the "legal and beneficial" owner who, under section 501(b) of the Copyright Act, "is entitled to institute an action for any infringement of that particular right committed while he or she is the owner of it." 17 U.S.C. § 501. This process might be straightforward. It might be the donor, if the works come from the artist or the artist's foundation. But the process might be more difficult: the artist might have conveyed intellectual property rights in certain artworks, as with Robert Indiana.[6] Or the artist might have directed that the intellectual property rights be transferred to a foundation upon death.

Identifying the owner is critical, because the owner controls how the image is used. This control could extend to every use described above. For example, while trademark law contains an exception to its infringement rules when someone displays an image of a work that is being sold, this exception has not been formally adopted into the copyright law.[7] Instead, the copyright law states that publication is permissible if the image being displayed depicts a work of art *in situ* where it is being sold.[8] This means that a gallery may freely post a picture of a work hanging on the gallery wall where it is being offered for sale, but the gallery faces the risk of litigation if it posts a reproduction of the artwork on its social media account. The same principle extends to museum catalogs and exhibitions, uses that require careful assessment under the Copyright Act, the fair-use law, and various other statutes and court decisions.[9] These intellectual property issues increase the risks and potential costs when accepting gifts of art, in addition to the costs that will be incurred to archive, display, and preserve the art itself.

After determining who owns the intellectual property rights, the museum should conduct background diligence about the rights holder. Has the owner permitted images of the works to be used before?[10] In what ways? Is there an existing edition of the catalogue raisonné that the museum intends to update?[11] Has the owner filed lawsuits or severely restricted the use of the images? The museum should ensure that its intentions for the gift square with the owner's approach to rights management.

Finally, before accepting a significant gift, around which the museum has extensive plans to use images of the art, the museum should consider speaking with the rights holder. If the rights holder is the donor, then the museum should seriously consider agreeing on a framework to govern how the images will be used. For example, if the museum has outlined specific programming or has other plans for using images of the artworks, it should attempt to obtain the required licenses to cover publication of the images.[12] Handling these details prospectively is often the wise strategy to avoid disputes and restrictions that may encumber a gift down the road.

If it is practically impossible to speak with the rights holder or, for various reasons, strategically unwise, then the museum should ensure that its background diligence on the owner and the rights does not present any red flags that call into question the viability of its plans.

Gifts of art are not free. Every museum knows that the works must be properly stored, conserved, and insured. But these are not the only important considerations that should inform a decision of whether to accept a proposed gift. The museum must also design a plan that allows for problem-free collateral use and reference to the works that accounts for the legal risks and financial constraints that are created by the fact that the copyright to the artwork does not transfer with the artwork itself.

Notes

1. Complaint, *Morgan Art Foundation Ltd. v. McKenzie et al*, No. 18 Civ. 4438(AT) (S.D.N.Y. May 18, 2018).

2. *Id.* at ¶¶ 43-53.

3. Amended Answer, Defenses & Counterclaim, *Morgan Art Foundation Ltd. et al v. James W. Brannan*, No. 18 Civ. 8231(AT-BCM) (May 29. 2019).

4. Complaint, *Morgan Art Foundation Ltd. et al v. James W. Brannan*, No. 18 Civ. 8231(UA) (S.D.N.Y. Sep. 11, 2018).

5. See Copyright Act, 17 U.S.C. § 202 (1976); see also, *Estate of Maier v. Goldstein*, No. 17 C 2951, 2017 WL 5569809, at *5 (N.D. Ill. Nov. 20, 2017) (holding that ownership of photographic negatives was distinct from ownership of the copyright to the artistic works embodied in those negatives); *Corcoran v. Sullivan*, 112 F.3d 836 (7th Cir. 1997) (ownership of a copyright, or of any of the exclusive rights under a copyright, is distinct from ownership of any material object in which the work is embodied).

6. See Daniel Grant, "The Bad Planning That Leaves So Many Artists' Estates Tangled in Lawsuits" (June 4, 2018), Observer.com, available at https://observer.com/2018/06/bad-planning-leads-artists-estates-to-become-tangled-in-lawsuits/.

7. Lanham Act, 15 U.S.C. § 1125 (2012) (using an image or trademark in an advertisement or promotion to allow consumers to compare goods and services is a fair use).

8. See *Stern v. Lavender*, 319 F. Supp. 3d 650, 682–83 (S.D.N.Y. 2018) (holding that the display of images online for the purpose of facilitating a legitimate sale of an object owned by the seller qualifies as fair use); *Rosen v. eBay, Inc.*, No. CV 13-6801 MWF EX, 2015 WL 1600081, at *19 (C.D. Cal. Jan. 16, 2015) (holding that the posting of magazine photographs to an online marketplace, as used to represent physical magazines for resale, constitutes fair use); *Teter v. Glass Onion, Inc.*, 723 F. Supp. 2d 1138, 1146 (W.D. Mo. 2010) (holding that a gallery owner had not infringed an artist's copyright by displaying the copyrighted works on the gallery's website for the purpose of advertising them for sale).

9. See Copyright Act, 17 U.S.C.A. § 113 (1976) (When a specific piece of art has been offered for sale or other distribution to the public, copyright does not include any right to prevent the making, distribution, or display of pictures or photographs of the piece in advertisements); see also Lanham Act, *supra* note 7. Under these statutes, the lawful owner and seller of a particular painting, photograph, sculpture, or other piece may use images of it specifically for the purpose of advertising it for sale, but not to promote attendance or patronage of a museum or gallery.

10. See Artists Rights Society, www.arsny.com (providing information on permissions for reproduction of visual art).

11. See International Foundation for Art Research, Catalogues Raisonnés, www.ifar. org/cat_rais.php (providing a searchable electronic database for published and forthcoming catalogues raisonnés).

12. See generally David M. Epstein, Eckstrom's Licensing in For. & Dom. Ops., § 5 Copyrights (Feb. 2019) (providing a general overview of copyright licensing law); Rachelle Brown & Maria Pallante-Hyun, To License or Not To License: A Look at Artists' Rights, Museum Practices & Institutional Risk, SJ049 A.L.I.-A.B.A. 511 (Mar. 24, 2004) (outlining risks faced by museums dealing with copyrighted works and comparing strategies for managing those risks); Kenneth D. Crews, *Museum Policies and Art Images: Conflicting Objectives and Copyright Overreaching*, 22 Fordham Intell. Prop. Media & Ent. L.J. 795 (2012) (identifying ambiguities in copyright law pertaining to images of artworks and exploring the challenges of museum policy making with respect to such images).

CHAPTER 25

Title Insurance as It Relates to Clear Title

ADAPTED BY SHARON S. THEOBALD

A RISK TO CLEAR TITLE can be present in all collecting catagories and genres and can impact the ability of the donor to give and the donee to receive a gift to museum's collection. Moreover, the legal liability for a title risk has potential exposure for museum trustees.

A challenge to title after the gift is made can cause a tax deduction to be set aside. Title regarding gifts of property is the possession of rights of ownership in that property. Separate rights of possession may include copyright interests, trademark rights, and any specific interest that previous owners may have reserved (adapted from Marie C. Malaro, *A Legal Primer on Managing Museum Collections*, 2nd edition). Ownership, therefore, includes a "bundle of rights" (*Black's Law Dictionary*). Bundle of rights is the concept that defines property ownership as a distinct and seperate right of the property owner, e.g., the right to use, to sell it, to lease it, to give it away, or to choose to exercise all or none of these rights (Garner, Bryan A., *Black's Law Dictionary*, 11th edition. Thomas Reuters, deluxe edition, 2019).

Title insurance is a form of protection. More detailed information is available on the ARIS Corporation website (www.aris-corporation.com).

Consider the following situation. Even some sophisticated collectors are surprised to learn of title insurance. Michael H. Steinhardt, retired hedge fund manager, philanthropist, and owner of one of the largest, most important antiquities collections in the world, didn't know such insurance existed when, in 1991, he bought an ancient golden platter called a phiale for $1.2 million (including commission) from a Swiss art dealer. His customs broker, when filling out the necessary forms, gave Switzerland as the country of origin. The phiale had in fact been found in Sicily.

The Italian government asked that it be returned. US Customs agents, armed with a warrant, showed up at Steinhardt's Fifth Avenue apartment and seized the platter. Though the Swiss dealer had signed a "terms of sale" agreement, he didn't have enough money to make good. Steinhardt was left holding the bag. Title insurance may have reimbursed his entire loss, including his litigation expenses. Moreover, the risk of an encumbered title can impact gifts of objects from antiquities to contemposrary art.

CHAPTER 26
Provenance and Provenance Research

MACKENZIE L. MALLON

PROVENANCE IS DEFINED AS the ownership history of an object from its creation to the present. The research and documentation of an object's provenance can help determine its legal ownership and are an integral part of a museum's commitment to make legal and ethical collecting decisions.

Museum collection-management policies often require provenance information be obtained from the donor, vendor, and/or through a museum's own research before an acquisition is finalized. The method of a museum's acquisition has no effect on an object's past provenance; therefore, understanding an object's provenance is just as important when an object is gifted to a museum as when one is acquired by purchase. Particular attention should be paid to the provenance of objects that fall within the following collection areas, as special consideration regarding the possibility of past looting or theft may apply:

- objects that could have changed hands in continental Europe during the Nazi era (1933–1945)

- works of ancient art and archaeological objects without documented provenance back to 1970 or evidence of legal import

- culturally sensitive objects, including Native American art and African art

The primary aim of provenance research is to document, as completely as possible, the names of previous owners, the dates of their ownership, the locations of their collections, the circumstances of an object's import into or export from countries between which it was transferred, and the method of transaction between and among each owner to the present.

Fully documenting an object's provenance can be a challenging task depending on the availability and reliability of documentation. Archival records may be lost or inaccessible; published references may contain incorrect or outdated information; former sellers may be unable or reluctant to reveal information because of privacy concerns. It may not always be possible to substantiate a complete provenance for an object; nonetheless, due diligence should be done in this research, taking care to document which resources have been consulted so future researchers are not required to duplicate past efforts.

Provenance research should begin with the object itself: document any marks, labels, stamps, or inscriptions that appear on the object. Request provenance information from the donor, including documentation of their own acquisition in the form of invoices, wills, import forms, and/or correspondence. Knowledge of how and from where an object was acquired by a presenting donor, in combination with any marks or labels on the object, are often standard starting points for provenance research. Since the history of every object is unique, the course of research may vary with each object. Additional steps may include identifying references to an object in published literature, accessing dealer or auction records, or locating archival inventories, among the many research sources.

For additional information, please consult Nancy H. Yeide, Konstantin Aldnsha, and Amy L. Walsh, *The AAM Guide to Provenance Research* (Washington, DC: American Association of Museums, 2001).

CHAPTER 27

Witnesses to World War II
Studies in Provenance Research

ROBERT B. SIMON

PROVENANCE RESEARCH CAN SEEM daunting to many. Teasing out the history of a work of art when its background may be long forgotten (either willfully or by neglect) may seem a tedious, if not impossible, quest. But its significance legally and culturally cannot be underestimated. And for those who become adept in it, the study of provenance can become an especially rewarding aspect of art-historical research.

The inanimate work of art that is before you—momentous or obscure as it might be—has been a witness to history, and tracing its travels, its ownership, its changing values can provide discerning insights into the past. The glories of aristocratic palaces, the horrors of wars, and the passions of great loves and lesser divorces as well as human dramas, bankruptcies, celebratory exhibitions, and desultory estate sales come alive through the mute observations that are the subject of your study.

Of course, it is the documentary aspects that have propelled information about provenance from an interesting footnote to an absolute necessity in the art world today. The chain of ownership—or even a few links in the chain—can establish good or bad title as well as authenticity. Works that have been acquired in good faith may have problematic pasts. Thorough research can restore or confirm authorship, patronage, dating, and historical connections. Responsibility rests with all those connected with a change of ownership—sellers and buyers, donors and donees, appraisers, and curators.

The method involved in provenance research, while specific to each object, is the same for all. It involves acquiring as much information as possible about a work's background and then pursuing the missing pieces. While some works may have been studied in the past, published, and thus accompanied by a dossier of sorts, others may arrive with no known history. It is the responsibility of the researcher, whatever his or her professional role might otherwise be, to obtain whatever information can be had from the previous owner, published sources, and, importantly, the object itself.

Unlike real estate, works of art generally travel around; therefore, documentation of a painting's history is often to be found on the work itself. The verso (reverse) of a painting may become something akin to a bulletin board over time: pages from obscure auction catalogues may be attached, exhibition and museum loan labels affixed, or inventory numbers elaborately inscribed. Three personal experiences may illustrate how crucial and how inconspicuous such information can be.

I: A Potential Auction Purchase

In 2005, a colleague and I noted an advertisement of an antique auction to be held in Rhode Island. Among the works offered was what looked to be an exquisite painting by the important nineteenth-century German painter Franz Xaver Winterhalter (1805–1873). The presale estimate, $40,000 to $60,000, was not inconsequential, but the painting's quality and rarity suggested a much higher value, so we decided to investigate.

The auctioneer gave the immediate provenance as that of a German baroness, but no earlier history was offered. However, at the auction preview we were able to examine the back of the painting, which featured a handwritten label in German giving basic information concerning the work (artist, dates, title, dimensions) followed by the cryptic line "Verst. Kat. Lempertz, Die Bestände der Galerie Stern - Düsseldorf, 1937. Abb. Taf. 1." A modest familiarity with the German language (and its abbreviations) was all that was needed to understand its meaning: "Lempertz Auction House catalogue, The Inventory of the Stern Gallery, Düsseldorf, 1937, Illustrated Plate 1." A visit to the Frick Art Reference Library, which held a copy of the Lempertz Catalogue, confirmed that the painting for sale was the same as the one in the 1937 auction in Düsseldorf. The import of this discovery was soon apparent. Max Stern, the owner of the Düsseldorf Gallery, was Jewish, and the referenced auction was one forced by the Nazi government as part of its Aryanization policy and as a requisite for Stern's ability to emigrate.

Today, Nazi forced sales are considered invalid and the equivalent of theft, and with only a day remaining before the auction, we alerted the Art Loss Register to our findings, as they maintain established relationships with policing authorities. The auction of the Winterhalter was halted, but the saga of the painting would take years to resolve as the consignor—whose father-in-law had purchased the painting at the 1937 sale—fled with the painting to Germany. Litigation in both the United States and Germany followed. In the end the painting was returned to Stern's heirs, who had established the nonprofit Max Stern Art Restitution Project to advance the cause of art restitution of its namesake and others similarly affected. Here one short handwritten line on the back of a painting led to the return of a highly important work of art.

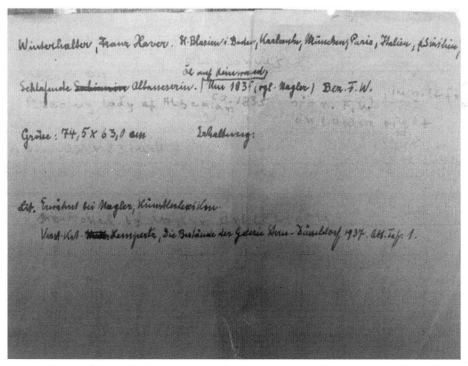

Figure 27.1.   Label with inscription on the verso of the Winterhalter painting, referencing the Stern auction of 1937. *Courtesy of Robert B. Simon*

II: An Appraisal

The front of another painting also revealed a problematic history. Photographs of *Prodigal Son* by the Antwerp artist Frans Francken III (1607–1667) had been sent to me for research and appraisal from a Texas collector. The owner's step-father had been a major in the US Army and, it was said, had won the painting and two others in a poker game while stationed in Germany after the war. Prominent on the frame was an engraved brass plaque giving the artist's name above the words "Joachim-Ernst Stiftung." That, investigation showed, was a foundation established in 1918 whose art holdings before the war had been on long-term deposit at various museums and historic houses in Dessau, Germany. A visit to the library confirmed that published catalogs listed the painting on view at the Anhalt Picture Gallery in Dessau until 1943. It had then been sent for safekeeping to the Solvayhall, a mine used as an art repository in the

Figure 27.2. Brass Plaque on the Frans Francken III painting, noting the "Joachim-Ernst Stiftung." *Courtesy of Robert B. Simon*

nearby town of Bernburg. At the conclusion of World War II, the painting was discovered missing; it was duly listed in the foundation's 2000 *Verlustkatalog*, a published catalog documenting its lost art holdings.

When informed of my research, the owner of the Frans Francken resisted both the news that his stepfather's painting was a stolen one and the fact that it should be returned—even after I confirmed its identity with the current director of the Anhalt Gallery. However, after seeing the movie *The Monuments Men*, which dramatized the efforts of American soldiers to protect European art during World War II, the owner had a change of heart and arranged for the painting's return to Dessau, where it, and the other two works, are again on view after more than seventy years. Here the plaque on the frame proved to be crucial.

III: A Consignment

A third example concerns a highly important painting by the Italian painter Parmigianino (1503–1540) received on consignment from a Massachusetts collector. This large work on a wood panel had been on loan to several prominent museums but had no published provenance despite its inclusion in a recent major loan exhibition. My library research soon led to the shocking discovery that the painting was illustrated in one of the photo albums documenting works of art intended for the Führermuseum, Hitler's planned picture gallery in Linz, Austria. It seems this significant painting was part of the most notorious and nefarious art plundering operation in history. Now it was imperative to discover how the picture came to be part of this assemblage of looted artworks and who its rightful owner might be. A call to the consignor, then quite elderly, was met with an almost casual response. He had forgotten to mention that he had inherited the painting from his parents, who had lived in Munich before the war. But they had spoken little of their wartime experience, and he was unsure of how the picture came to be owned by them.

The Nazis were extraordinary record keepers, and with the aid of a series of otherwise innocuous-looking ink labels, inscriptions, and inventory numbers still intact on the verso of the panel, I was able to reconstruct its journey through World War II. To do so, I consulted the detailed records kept at the Deutsches Historisches Museum in Berlin and the National Archives in Washington—all now digitized and available, quite astonishingly, online (the American ones from the Ardelia Hall Collection, courtesy of the website fold3.com).

The Ardelia Ripley Hall Archives are housed in the collection of the National Archives at College Park, Maryland, "The Ardelia Hall Collection" includes the records of the Roberts Commission, field reports of the Monuments Men, minutes from international conferences, over 50,000 photographic property cards from the Munich Central Collecting Point, and much more. https://www.monumentsmenfoundation.org/hall-ardelia-r. This integral collection of records was named in honor of Adelia Hall, who laboriously organized and maintained them while working at the U.S. Department of State both during and after World War II. Also, Fold3 has digitized this material and makes it available freely on their website https://www.fold3.com/title/755/ardelia-hall-collection-omgus-records.

The documentation was both rewarding and frightening. I was able to read about not only the arrest of the owner's father at his Munich home on Kristallnacht in 1938 but also the seizure of his art collection a week later and its expropriation and eventual sale to Hitler. I traced the painting's journey through Nazi storage depots until it reached the infamous salt mines at Alt Aussee. There it joined some of the greatest art treasures of Europe—a Leonardo painting, a Michelangelo sculpture, Van Eyck's *Ghent Altarpiece*, among the most celebrated—until the conclusion of the war. The painting was recovered by the Allies, returned to Munich, and eventually restituted to the owner, who had emigrated to the United States. Here was a précis of a Holocaust family saga told through the travels of a single painting.

While the painting at first seemed to be under the cloud of Nazi looting, the research established that it had good and clear title. Moreover, the family's written request to the Allied authorities for restitution revealed from whom they had acquired the painting, providing another link in the chain of ownership, one that further research would later be able to connect with the work's earlier documented history. The painting's unbroken provenance is now established from the year 1603 until today.

Figure 27.3. Numbers with meaning on the verso of the Parmigianino painting. Top: "K.1288" was the inventory number assigned to the painting at the Nazi storage depot at the Abbey of Kremsmünster in 1942. Below: "2554" was the number given the painting when it was transferred for storage to the Führerbau in Munich in 1943. *Courtesy of Robert B. Simon*

Figure 27.4. (shares caption with figure 27.3). *Courtesy of Robert B. Simon*

These three examples highlight the importance of careful scrutiny of a work of art, with focused attention beyond that which an art historian, student, or critic of the work might normally undertake. More like a crime-scene investigator than an aesthete, the researcher in such situations needs to examine the painting's verso, its frame, and stretcher bars, searching for labels, inscriptions, chalk marks, storage numbers, stamps, and stencils—anything that may evidence earlier ownership. These may serve as signposts along the often long and fraught route that a work of art has traveled.

Part Six

Tax Perspectives for Museums

Review of Changes to the
Pension Protection Act
(IRS Notice 2006-96)

CHAPTER 28
Related and Unrelated Use

COMPILED AND EDITED BY LAURETTE E. MCCARTHY

THE IRS REFERS TO GIFS of tangible personal property as property other than land or buildings that can be seen or touched. It includes furniture, books, jewelry, paintings, and cars that can be donated for tax pruposes. The major distinction herin is Unrelated Use. The term "unrelated use" means a use unrelated to the exempt purpose or fuction of the charitable organization. For example, if a painting contributed to an educational institution is used by that organization for educational purposes by being placed in its library for display and study by art students, the use isn't an unrelated use. But if the painting is sold and the proceeds are used by the organization for educational purposes, the use is an unrelated use and IRS Form 8282 must be provided by the donee to the donor. In IRS.gov/Pub526, IRS Publication 526 (2018) Charitable Contributions

- The use of the property by the donee (nonprofit) organization must be related to the purpose or function of the donee's tax exemption.

- This means that the property gifted cannot be converted (sold) from the form of the gift (for three years) even if the proceeds of the conversion are used in the context of the donee's 501 (c) (3) charter.

- The museum must keep and use the donated object for at least three years in order for the donor to take the full fair market value deduction on their taxes. (Previously, museums had to hold and make use of the object for two years.)

- If the museum intends to sell the donated object, they must check the "Unrelated Use" box on Form 8283.

- If the museum accepts the object donated, but then sells before three years, the donated object becomes unrelated to the use of the museum.

- Exception allows donee, under penalty of perjury, to make "certification" that the use of the property by the donee was substantial and related to the donee's charitable purpose and describes how the property was used and how it furthered the donee's charitable purpose, or states the intended use by the donee at the time of the contribution and certifies that the intended use has become impossible or unfeasible to implement.

- If the museum sells before three years, it must file IRS Form 8282 and send a copy to the donor.

CHAPTER 29

Penalties for Donees

COMPILED AND EDITED BY LAURETTE E. MCCARTHY

THE FOLLOWING TEXT COMES from page 3 of the general instructions for IRS Form 8282:

> Failure-to-file penalty. The organization may be subject to a penalty if it fails to file this form by the due date, fails to include all of the information required to be shown on the filed form, or includes incorrect information on the filed form. The penalty is generally $50 per form. For more details, see sections 6721 and 6724.
>
> Fraudulent identification of exempt use property. A $10,000 penalty may apply to any person who identifies in part III tangible personal property the organization sold, exchanged, or otherwise disposed of, as having a use that is related to a purpose or function knowing that such property was not intended for such a use. For more details, see section 6720B.

CHAPTER 30
Penalties for Donors for Related and Unrelated Gifts of Property

COMPILED AND EDITED BY LAURETTE E. MCCARTHY

UNDER SECTION 170(E)(7) (added in 2006 by the Pension Protection Act), if the museum (donee) sells before three years, then the donor has to recapture (take into income) the amount of the deduction taken in excess of the donor's basis of the property at the time of the contribution.

You must recapture part of your charitable contribution deduction by including it in your income if all the following statements are true:

1. You donate tangible personal property with a claimed value of more than $5,000, and your deduction is more than your basis in the property.

2. The organization sells, trades, or otherwise disposes of the property after the year it was contributed but within three years of the contribution.

3. The organization does not provide a written statement (such as on Form 8282, part IV), signed by an officer of the organization under penalty of perjury, that either

   a. certifies its use of the property was substantial and related to the organization's purpose, or

   b. certifies its intended use of the property became impossible.

If all the preceding statements are true, include in your income

1. the deduction you claimed for the property, minus

2. your basis in the property when you made the contribution.

Include this amount in your income for the year the qualified organization disposes of the property. Report the recaptured amount on Form 1040, line 21.

You may be liable for a penalty if you overstate the value or adjusted basis of donated property.

- 20% penalty. The penalty is 20% of the underpayment of tax related to the overstatement if: The value or adjusted basis claimed on the return is 150% or more of the correct amount, and You underpaid your tax by more than $5,000 because of the overstatement.

- 40% penalty. The penalty is 40%, rather than 20%, if: The value or adjusted basis claimed on the return is 200% or more of the correct amount, and You underpaid your tax by more than $5,000 because of the overstatement. IRS Publication 561. Revised February 2020, p. 11.

Recapture of Deduction

You must recapture your charitable contribution deduction by including it in your income if both of the following statements are true:

1. You contributed a fractional interest in tangible personal property after August 17, 2006.

2. You do not contribute the rest of your interests in the property to a qualified organization on or before the earlier of

a. the date that is ten years after the date of the initial contribution, or

b. the date of your death.

Recapture is also required in any case in which the qualified organization has not taken substantial physical possession of the property and has not used it in a way related to its purpose during the period beginning on the date of the initial fractional contribution and ending on the earlier of

a. the date that is ten years after the date of the initial contribution, or

b. the date of your death.

Additional Tax

If you must recapture your deduction, you must also pay interest and an additional tax equal to 10 percent of the amount recaptured.

CHAPTER 31
Penalties for Appraisers

COMPILED AND EDITED BY LAURETTE E. MCCARTHY

SECTION 1219 OF THE PENSION PROTECTION ACT of 2006 added IRC 6695A, *Substanial and Gross Valuation Misstatements Attributable to Incorrect Appraisals*. This penalty provision allows the IRS to assert a penalty against any person who prepared an appraisal of the value of property and who knew, or reasonably should have known, the appraisal would be used in connection with a return or claim for refund and that appraisal results in a substantial valuation misstatement (within the meaning of IRC 6662[e]), a substantial estate or gift tax vaulation understatement (within the meaning of IRC 6662[g]), or a gross valuation misstatement (within the meaning of IRC 6662[h]) with respect to such property. Note IRS 20.1.12.1 (12/18/2017).

Specifically, the following penalties apply for appraisers who issue substantial or gross valuation misstatements attributable to incorrect appraisals.

- The new Declaration of the Appraiser furthermore states that the appraiser understands "that a substantial or gross valuation misstatement resulting from the appraisal of the value of the property that I know, or reasonably should know, would be used in connection with a return or claim for refund, may subject me to the penalty under section 6695A."

An appraiser who prepares an incorrect appraisal may have to pay a penalty if

1. the appraiser knows or should have known the appraisal would be used in connection with a return or claim for refund, and

2. the appraisal results in the 20 percent or 40 percent penalty for a valuation misstatement described later under penalty. The penalty imposed on the appraiser is the smaller of these two figures:

    a. The greater of

        i. 10 percent of the underpayment due to the misstatement, or

        ii. $1,000, or

    b. 125 percent of the gross income received for the appraisal.

In addition, any appraiser who falsely or fraudulently overstates the value of property described in a qualified appraisal of a Form 8283 that the appraiser has signed may be subject to a civil penalty for aiding and abetting an understatement of tax liability and may have his or her appraisal disregarded.

CHAPTER 32

Fractional Gifts/ Partial Interest Gifts
Gifts Made for Tax Purposes

COMPILED AND EDITED BY LAURETTE E. MCCARTHY

FRACTIONAL GIFTS OCCUR when donors gift a specific interest in an object over a period of time and thus are required to have an appraisal completed for each year of the fractional gift.

- You donate a work of art over a period of time and have an appraisal done every year.

- Subsequent gifting is limited to the lesser of the initial FMV contribution or the later FMV contribution.

- So, if the FMV increases, you cannot take the larger deduction.

- But if the FMV decreases, you must take the lower deduction.

- Gift must be completed within the earlier of ten years or death of taxpayer.

- Donee must take substantial physical possession or make use of the property.

- If any of the above stated conditions are not met, then the deduction previously taken will be recaptured with interest.

CHAPTER 33
Charity Auctions and Donation Deductions

COMPILED AND EDITED BY LAURETTE E. MCCARTHY

DONORS WHO PURCHASE ITEMS at a charity auction may claim a charitable contribution deduction for the excess of the purchase price paid for an item over its fair market value. The donor must be able to show, however, that he or she knew that the value of the item was less than the amount paid. For example, a charity may publish a catalogue, given to each person who attends an auction, providing a good faith estimate of items that will be available for bidding. Assuming the donor has no reason to doubt the accuracy of the published estimate, if he or she pays more than the published value, the difference between the amount paid and the published value may constitute a charitable contribution deduction.

In addition, donors who provide goods for charities to sell at an auction often ask the charity if the donor is entitled to claim a fair market value charitable deduction for a contribution of appreciated property to the charity that will later be sold. Under these circumstances, the law limits a donor's charitable deduction to the donor's tax basis in the contributed property and does not permit the donor to claim a fair market value charitable deduction for the contribution.

Specifically, the Treasury Regulations under section 170 provide that if a donor contributes tangible personal property to a charity that is put to an *unrelated use*, the donor's contribution is limited to the donor's tax basis in the contributed property.

The term unrelated use means a use that is unrelated to the charity's exempt purposes or function, or, in the case of a governmental unit, a use of the contributed property for other than exclusively public purposes. The sale of an item is considered unrelated, even if the sale raises money for the charity to use in its programs.

CHAPTER 34

IRS Definitions of a Qualified Appraisal and Qualified Appraiser (Effective January 1, 2019)

§ 1.170A–17 Qualified Appraisal and Qualified Appraiser.

(a) *Qualified appraisal—*

(1) *Definition.* For purposes of section 170(f)(11) and § 1.170A–16(d)(1)(ii) and (e)(1)(ii), the term *qualified appraisal* means an appraisal document that is prepared by a qualified appraiser (as defined in paragraph (b)(1) of this section) in accordance with generally accepted appraisal standards (as defined in paragraph (a)(2) of this section) and otherwise complies with the requirements of this paragraph (a).

(2) *Generally accepted appraisal standards defined.* For purposes of paragraph (a)(1) of this section, *generally accepted appraisal standards* means the substance and principles of the Uniform Standards of Professional Appraisal Practice, as developed by the Appraisal Standards Board of the Appraisal Foundation.

(3) *Contents of qualified appraisal.* A qualified appraisal must include—

(i) The following information about the contributed property:

(A) A description in sufficient detail under the circumstances, taking into account the value of the property, for a person who is not generally familiar with the type of property to ascertain that the appraised property is the contributed property.

(B) In the case of real property or tangible personal property, the condition of the property.

(C) The valuation effective date, as defined in paragraph (a)(5)(i) of this section.

(D) The fair market value, within the meaning of § 1.170A–1(c)(2), of the contributed property on the valuation effective date;

(ii) The terms of any agreement or understanding by or on behalf of the donor and donee that relates to the use, sale, or other disposition of the contributed property, including, for example, the terms of any agreement or understanding that—

(A) Restricts temporarily or permanently a donee's right to use or dispose of the contributed property;

(B) Reserves to, or confers upon, anyone, other than a donee or an organization participating with a donee in cooperative fund-raising, any right to the income from the contributed property or to the possession of the property, including the right to vote contributed securities, to acquire the property by purchase or otherwise, or to designate the person having income, possession, or right to acquire; or

(C) Earmarks contributed property for a particular use;

(iii) The date, or expected date, of the contribution to the donee;

(iv) The following information about the appraiser:

(A) Name, address, and taxpayer identification number.

(B) Qualifications to value the type of property being valued, including the appraiser's education and experience.

(C) If the appraiser is acting in his or her capacity as a partner in a partnership, an employee of any person, whether an individual, corporation, or partnership, or an independent contractor engaged by a person other than the donor, the name, address, and taxpayer identification number of the partnership or the person who employs or engages the qualified appraiser;

(v) The signature of the appraiser and the date signed by the appraiser (appraisal report date);

(vi) The following declaration by the appraiser: "I understand that my appraisal will be used in connection with a return or claim for refund. I also understand that, if there is a substantial or gross valuation misstatement of the value of the property claimed on the return or claim for refund that is based on my appraisal, I may be subject to a penalty under section 6695A of the Internal Revenue

Code, as well as other applicable penalties. I affirm that I have not been at any time in the three-year period ending on the date of the appraisal barred from presenting evidence or testimony before the Department of the Treasury or the Internal Revenue Service pursuant to 31 U.S.C. section 330(c)";

(vii) A statement that the appraisal was prepared for income tax purposes;(viii) The method of valuation used to determine the fair market value, such as the income approach, the market-data approach, or the replacement-cost-less-depreciation approach; and

(ix) The specific basis for the valuation, such as specific comparable sales transactions or statistical sampling, including a justification for using sampling and an explanation of the sampling procedure employed.

(4) *Timely appraisal report.* A qualified appraisal must be signed and dated by the qualified appraiser no earlier than sixty days before the date of the contribution and no later than—

(i) The due date, including extensions, of the return on which the deduction for the contribution is first claimed;

(ii) In the case of a donor that is a partnership or S corporation, the due date, including extensions, of the return on which the deduction for the contribution is first reported; or

(iii) In the case of a deduction first claimed on an amended return, the date on which the amended return is filed.

(5) *Valuation effective date—*

(i) *Definition.* The *valuation effective date* is the date to which the value opinion applies.

(ii) *Timely valuation effective date.* For an appraisal report dated before the date of the contribution, as described in § 1.170A–1(b), the valuation effective date must be no earlier than sixty days before the date of the contribution and no later than the date of the contribution. For an appraisal report dated on or after the date of the contribution, the valuation effective date must be the date of the contribution.

(6) *Exclusion for donor knowledge of falsity.* An appraisal is not a qualified appraisal for a particular contribution, even if the requirements of this paragraph

(a) are met, if the donor either failed to disclose or misrepresented facts, and a reasonable person would expect that this failure or misrepresentation would cause the appraiser to misstate the value of the contributed property.

(7) *Number of appraisals required.* A donor must obtain a separate qualified appraisal for each item of property for which an appraisal is required under section 170(f)(11)(C) and (D) and paragraph (d) or (e) of § 1.170A–16 and that is not included in a group of similar items of property, as defined in § 1.170A–13(c)(7)(iii). For rules regarding the number of appraisals required if similar items of property are contributed, see section 170(f)(11)(F) and § 1.170A–13(c)(3)(iv)(A).

(8) *Time of receipt of qualified appraisal.* The qualified appraisal must be received by the donor before the due date, including extensions, of the return on which a deduction is first claimed, or reported in the case of a donor that is a partnership or S corporation, under section 170 with respect to the donated property, or, in the case of a deduction first claimed, or reported, on an amended return, the date on which the return is filed.

(9) *Prohibited appraisal fees.* The fee for a qualified appraisal cannot be based to any extent on the appraised value of the property. For example, a fee for an appraisal will be treated as based on the appraised value of the property if any part of the fee depends on the amount of the appraised value that is allowed by the Internal Revenue Service after an examination.

(10) *Retention of qualified appraisal.* The donor must retain the qualified appraisal for so long as it may be relevant in the administration of any internal revenue law.

(11) *Effect of appraisal disregarded pursuant to 31 U.S.C. section 330(c).* If an appraiser has been prohibited from practicing before the Internal Revenue Service by the Secretary under 31 U.S.C. section 330(c) at any time during the three-year period ending on the date the appraisal is signed by the appraiser, any appraisal prepared by the appraiser will be disregarded as to value, but could constitute a qualified appraisal if the requirements of this section are otherwise satisfied, and the donor had no knowledge that the signature, date, or declaration was false when the appraisal and Form 8283 (section B) were signed by the appraiser.

(12) *Partial interest.* If the contributed property is a partial interest, the appraisal must be of the partial interest.

(b) *Qualified appraiser—*

(1) *Definition.* For purposes of section 170(f)(11) and § 1.170A–16(d)(1)(ii) and (e)(1)(ii), the term *qualified appraiser* means an individual with verifiable education and experience in valuing the type of property for which the appraisal is performed, as described in paragraphs (b)(2) through (4) of this section.

(2) *Education and experience in valuing the type of property—*

(i) *In general.* An individual is treated as having education and experience in valuing the type of property within the meaning of paragraph (b)(1) of this section if, as of the date the individual signs the appraisal, the individual has—

(A) Successfully completed (for example, received a passing grade on a final examination) professional or college-level coursework, as described in paragraph (b)(2)(ii) of this section, in valuing the type of property, as described in paragraph (b)(3) of this section, and has two or more years of experience in valuing the type of property, as described in paragraph (b)(3) of this section; or

(B) Earned a recognized appraiser designation, as described in paragraph (b)(2)(iii) of this section, for the type of property, as described in paragraph (b)(3) of this section.

(ii) *Coursework must be obtained from an educational organization, generally recognized professional trade or appraiser organization, or employer educational program.* For purposes of paragraph (b)(2)(i)(A) of this section, the coursework must be obtained from—

(A) A professional or college-level educational organization described in section 170(b)(1)(A)(ii);

(B) A generally recognized professional trade or appraiser organization that regularly offers educational programs in valuing the type of property; or

(C) An employer as part of an employee apprenticeship or educational program substantially similar to the educational programs described in paragraphs (b)(2)(ii)(A) and (B) of this section.

(iii) *Recognized appraiser designation defined.* A *recognized appraiser designation* means a designation awarded by a generally recognized professional appraiser organization on the basis of demonstrated competency.

(3) *Type of property defined—*

(i) *In general.* The type of property means the category of property customary in the appraisal field for an appraiser to value.

(ii) *Examples.* The following examples illustrate the rule of paragraphs (b)(2)(i) and (b)(3)(i) of this section:

Example (1). Coursework in valuing type of property. There are very few professional-level courses offered in widget appraising, and it is customary in the appraisal field for personal property appraisers to appraise widgets. Appraiser *A* has successfully completed professional-level coursework in valuing personal property generally but has completed no coursework in valuing widgets. The coursework completed by appraiser *A* is for the type of property under paragraphs (b)(2)(i) and (b)(3)(i) of this section.

Example (2). Experience in valuing type of property. It is customary for professional antique appraisers to appraise antique widgets. Appraiser *B* has two years of experience in valuing antiques generally and is asked to appraise an antique widget. Appraiser *B* has obtained experience in valuing the type of property under paragraphs (b)(2)(i) and (b)(3)(i) of this section.

Example (3). No experience in valuing type of property. It is not customary for professional antique appraisers to appraise new widgets. Appraiser *C* has experience in appraising antiques generally but no experience in appraising new widgets. Appraiser *C* is asked to appraise a new widget. Appraiser *C* does not have experience in valuing the type of property under paragraphs (b)(2)(i) and (b)(3)(i) of this section.

(4) *Verifiable.* For purposes of paragraph (b)(1) of this section, education and experience in valuing the type of property are verifiable if the appraiser specifies in the appraisal the appraiser's education and experience in valuing the type of property, as described in paragraphs (b)(2) and (3) of this section, and the appraiser makes a declaration in the appraisal that, because of the appraiser's education and experience, the appraiser is qualified to make appraisals of the type of property being valued.

(5) *Individuals who are not qualified appraisers.* The following individuals are not qualified appraisers for the appraised property:

(i) An individual who receives a fee prohibited by paragraph (a)(9) of this section for the appraisal of the appraised property.

(ii) The donor of the property.

(iii) A party to the transaction in which the donor acquired the property (for example, the individual who sold, exchanged, or gave the property to the donor, or any individual who acted as an agent for the transferor or for the donor for the sale, exchange, or gift), unless the property is contributed within two months of the date of acquisition and its appraised value does not exceed its acquisition price.

(iv) The donee of the property.

(v) Any individual who is either—

(A) Related, within the meaning of section 267(b), to, or an employee of, an individual described in paragraph (b)(5)(ii), (iii), or (iv) of this section;

(B) Married to an individual described in paragraph (b)(5)(v)(A) of this section; or

(C) An independent contractor who is regularly used as an appraiser by any of the individuals described in paragraph (b)(5)(ii), (iii), or (iv) of this section, and who does not perform a majority of his or her appraisals for others during the taxable year.

(vi) An individual who is prohibited from practicing before the Internal Revenue Service by the secretary under 31 U.S.C. section 330(c) at any time during the three-year period ending on the date the appraisal is signed by the individual.

(c) *Effective/applicability date.* This section applies to contributions made on or after January 1, 2019. Taxpayers may rely on the rules of this section for appraisals prepared for returns or submissions filed after August 17, 2006.

CHAPTER 35

IRS Art Advisory Panel

COMPILED AND EDITED BY LAURETTE E. MCCARTHY

THE PANEL HELPS IRS REVIEW and evaluate property appraisals submitted by taxpayers in support of the fair market value claimed for works of art included in federal income, estate and gift tax cases in accordance with the Internal Revenue Code. The panel members, up to twenty-five renowned art experts, serve without compensation.

Annual Summary Report: The Annual Summary Report describes the closed meeting activity of the Commissioner's Art Advisory Panel for the most recent year. The report discusses the procedures of the Art Panel, provides a list of panelists and summarizes the art items reviewed during the year. If you would like older Annual Summary Reports, please contact the director, Art Appraisal Services 305-982-5364.

Publications

- Publication 526. Charitable Contributions (PDF)

- Publication 561, Determining the Value of Donated Property (PDF). Designed to help donors and appraisers determine the value of property that is given to qualified organizations. It includes the kind of information you must have to support your decision.

CHAPTER 36

IRS Art Advisory Panel Format for Gifts over $50,000

COMPILED AND EDITED BY LAURETTE E. MCCARTHY

ALL TAXPAYER CASES SELECTED FOR examination that include an item of art with a claimed value of $50,000 or more must be referred to Art Appraisal Services for possible review by the Commissioner's Art Advisory Panel (see IRM 4.48.2 and IRM 8.18.1.3). Please review the photographic requirements for referrals and also our preferred individual appraisal item format (PDF) for works of art valued at over $50,000. For general inquiries, contact director, Art Appraisal Services at 305-982-5364.

Internal Revenue Service/Art Appraisal Services

1111 Constitution Ave., Suite 700

CAP:SO:ART

Washington, DC 20224-0002

ATTN: AAS

Note well:

- Gifts exceeding $50,000 are automatically reviewed by the IRS Art Advisory panel; this is a change from the previous automatic review of donations exceeding $20,000.

- Photographic requirements have been revised to allow submission of professional-quality digital images as well as or instead of 35mm professional-quality images.

- Appraisals for gifts exceeding $20,000 should follow the format recommended by the IRS Art Advisory Panel, available at www.irs.gov.

IRS Relevant Publications

- Publication 526, Charitable Contributions

- Publication 561, Determining the Value of Donated Property. Designed to help donors and appraisers determine the value of property that is given to qualified organizations. It includes specific information that a donor must have to support gifts and donations.

CHAPTER 37
IRS Forms

COMPILED AND EDITED BY LAURETTE E. MCCARTHY

Form 8283, Non-Cash Charitable Contributions. This form is filed with the taxpayer's return (see chapter 12).

Form 8282, Donee Information Return. Filed by donee (museum) upon sale of property. Form 8282 is another IRS form that may be associated with charitable contributions. Donors may receive this form from the donee if the asset has a fair market value of more than $500 and is disposed of within three years. If these condition are met, donees should provide Form 8282 to donors and the IRS.

IRS Form: Preferred Object Identification Format for Art* Valued over $50,000

IRS Publication 561: Determining the Value of Donated Property

Donee Information Return

(Sale, Exchange, or Other Disposition of Donated Property)

▶ See instructions.

OMB No. 1545-0908

Give a Copy to Donor

Parts To Complete

- If the organization is an **original donee,** complete *Identifying Information,* Part I (lines 1a–1d and, if applicable, lines 2a–2d), and Part III.
- If the organization is a **successor donee,** complete *Identifying Information,* Part I, Part II, and Part III.

Identifying Information

Print or Type	Name of charitable organization (donee)	Employer identification number
	Address (number, street, and room or suite no.) (or P.O. box no. if mail is not delivered to the street address)	
	City or town, state, and ZIP code	

Part I — Information on ORIGINAL DONOR and SUCCESSOR DONEE Receiving the Property

1a Name of original donor of the property	1b Identifying number(s)
1c Address (number, street, and room or suite no.) (P.O. box no. if mail is not delivered to the street address)	
1d City or town, state, and ZIP code	

Note. Complete lines 2a–2d only if the organization gave this property to another charitable organization (successor donee).

2a Name of charitable organization	2b Employer identification number
2c Address (number, street, and room or suite no.) (or P.O. box no. if mail is not delivered to the street address)	
2d City or town, state, and ZIP code	

Part II — Information on PREVIOUS DONEES. Complete this part only if the organization was not the first donee to receive the property. See the instructions before completing lines 3a through 4d.

3a Name of original donee	3b Employer identification number
3c Address (number, street, and room or suite no.) (or P.O. box no. if mail is not delivered to the street address)	
3d City or town, state, and ZIP code	

4a Name of preceding donee	4b Employer identification number
4c Address (number, street, and room or suite no.) (or P.O. box no. if mail is not delivered to the street address)	
4d City or town, state, and ZIP code	

For Paperwork Reduction Act Notice, see page 4.   Cat. No. 62307Y   Form **8282** (Rev. 4-2009)

Figure 37.1.   Form 8282

| **Part III** | **Information on DONATED PROPERTY** |

	1. Description of the donated property sold, exchanged, or otherwise disposed of and how the organization used the property. (If you need more space, attach a separate statement.)	**2.** Did the disposition involve the organization's entire interest in the property?		**3.** Was the use related to the organization's exempt purpose or function?		**4.** Information on use of property. • If you answered "Yes" to question 3 and the property was tangible personal property, describe how the organization's use of the property furthered its exempt purpose or function. Also complete Part IV below. • If you answered "No" to question 3 and the property was tangible personal property, describe the organization's intended use (if any) at the time of the contribution. Also complete Part IV below, if the intended use at the time of the contribution was related to the organization's exempt purpose or function and it became impossible or infeasible to implement.
		Yes	No	Yes	No	
A						
B						
C						
D						

		Donated Property			
		A	**B**	**C**	**D**
5	Date the organization received the donated property (MM/DD/YY)	/ /	/ /	/ /	/ /
6	Date the original donee received the property (MM/DD/YY)	/ /	/ /	/ /	/ /
7	Date the property was sold, exchanged, or otherwise disposed of (MM/DD/YY)	/ /	/ /	/ /	/ /
8	Amount received upon disposition	$	$	$	$

| **Part IV** | **Certification** |

You must sign the certification below if any property described in Part III above is tangible personal property and:

• You answered "Yes" to question 3 above, or

• You answered "No" to question 3 above and the intended use of the property became impossible or infeasible to implement.

Under penalties of perjury and the penalty under section 6720B, I certify that either: (1) the use of the property that meets the above requirements, and is described above in Part III, was substantial and related to the donee organization's exempt purpose or function; or (2) the donee organization intended to use the property for its exempt purpose or function, but the intended use has become impossible or infeasible to implement.

▶ _____   ▶ _____
Signature of officer   Title   Date

Sign Here

Under penalties of perjury, I declare that I have examined this return, including accompanying schedules and statements, and to the best of my knowledge and belief, it is true, correct, and complete.

▶ _____   ▶ _____
Signature of officer   Title   Date

_____
Type or print name

Form **8282** (Rev. 4-2009)

Figure 37.1. *(continued)*

General Instructions

Section references are to the Internal Revenue Code.

Purpose of Form

Donee organizations use Form 8282 to report information to the IRS and donors about dispositions of certain charitable deduction property made within 3 years after the donor contributed the property.

Definitions

 For Form 8282 and these instructions, the term "donee" includes all donees, unless specific reference is made to "original" or "successor" donees.

Original donee. The first donee to or for which the donor gave the property. The original donee is required to sign Form 8283, Noncash Charitable Contributions, *Section B. Donated Property Over $5,000 (Except Certain Publicly Traded Securities),* presented by the donor for charitable deduction property.

Successor donee. Any donee of property other than the original donee.

Charitable deduction property. Any donated property (other than money and publicly traded securities) if the claimed value exceeds $5,000 per item or group of similar items donated by the donor to one or more donee organizations. This is the property listed in Section B on Form 8283.

Who Must File

Original and successor donee organizations must file Form 8282 if they sell, exchange, consume, or otherwise dispose of (with or without consideration) charitable deduction property (or any portion) within 3 years after the date the original donee received the property. See *Charitable deduction property* above.

If the organization sold, exchanged, or otherwise disposed of motor vehicles, airplanes, or boats, see Pub. 526, Charitable Contributions.

Exceptions. There are two situations where Form 8282 does not have to be filed.

1. Items valued at $500 or less. The organization does not have to file Form 8282 if, at the time the original donee signed Section B of Form 8283, the donor had signed a statement on Form 8283 that the appraised value of the specific item was not more than $500. If Form 8283 contains more than one item, this exception applies only to those items that are clearly identified as having a value of $500 or less. However, for purposes of the donor's determination of whether the appraised value of the item exceeds $500, all shares of nonpublicly traded stock, or items that form a set, are considered one item. For example, a collection of books written by the same

author, components of a stereo system, or six place settings of a pattern of silverware are considered one item.

2. Items consumed or distributed for charitable purpose. The organization does not have to file Form 8282 if an item is consumed or distributed, without consideration, in fulfilling your purpose or function as a tax-exempt organization. For example, no reporting is required for medical supplies consumed or distributed by a tax-exempt relief organization in aiding disaster victims.

When To File

If the organization disposes of charitable deduction property within 3 years of the date the original donee received it and the organization does not meet exception 1 or 2 above, the organization must file Form 8282 within 125 days after the date of disposition.

Exception. If the organization did not file because it had no reason to believe the substantiation requirements applied to the donor, but the organization later becomes aware that the substantiation requirements did apply, the organization must file Form 8282 within 60 days after the date it becomes aware it was liable. For example, this exception would apply where Section B of Form 8283 is furnished to a successor donee after the date that donee disposes of the charitable deduction property.

Missing information. If Form 8282 is filed by the due date, enter the organization's name, address, and employer identification number (EIN) and complete at least Part III, columns 1, 2, 3, and 4; and Part IV. The organization does not have to complete the remaining items if the information is not available. For example, the organization may not have the information necessary to complete all entries if the donor did not make Section B of Form 8283 available.

Where To File

Send Form 8282 to the Department of Treasury, Internal Revenue Service Center, Ogden, UT 84201-0027.

Other Requirements

Information the organization must give a successor donee. If the property is transferred to another charitable organization within the 3-year period discussed earlier, the organization must give the successor donee all of the following information.

1. The name, address, and EIN of the organization.

2. A copy of Section B of Form 8283 that the organization received from the donor or a preceding donee. The preceding donee is the one who gave the organization the property.

3. A copy of this Form 8282, within 15 days after the organization files it.

The organization must furnish items 1 and 2 above within 15 days after the latest of the date:

● The organization transferred the property,

● The original donee signed Section B of Form 8283, or

● The organization received a copy of Section B of Form 8283 from the preceding donee if the organization is also a successor donee.

Information the successor donee must give the organization. The successor donee organization to whom the organization transferred this property is required to give the organization its name, address, and EIN within 15 days after the later of:

● The date the organization transferred the property, or

● The date the successor donee received a copy of Section B of Form 8283.

Information the organization must give the donor. The organization must give a copy of Form 8282 to the original donor of the property.

Recordkeeping. The organization must keep a copy of Section B of Form 8283 in its records.

Penalties

Failure to file penalty. The organization may be subject to a penalty if it fails to file this form by the due date, fails to include all of the information required to be shown on the filed form, or includes incorrect information on the filed form. The penalty is generally $50 per form. For more details, see section 6721 and 6724.

Fraudulent identification of exempt use property. A $10,000 penalty may apply to any person who identifies in Part III tangible personal property the organization sold, exchanged, or otherwise disposed of, as having a use that is related to a purpose or function knowing that such property was not intended for such use. For more details, see section 6720B.

Specific Instructions

Part I

Line 1a. Enter the name of the original donor.

Line 1b. The donor's identifying number may be either an employer identification number or a social security number, and should be the same number provided on page 2 of Form 8283.

Line 1c and 1d. Enter the last known address of the original donor.

Lines 2a–2d. Complete these lines if the organization gave the property to another charitable organization successor donee (defined earlier). If the organization is an original donee, skip Part II and go to Part III.

Figure 37.1. *(continued)*

Part II

Complete Part II only if the organization is a successor donee. If the organization is the original donee, do not complete any lines in Part II; go directly to Part III.

If the organization is the **second donee**, complete lines 3a through 3d. If the organization is the **third or later donee,** complete lines 3a through 4d. On lines 4a through 4d, give information on the preceding donee.

Part III

Column 1. For charitable deduction property that the organization sold, exchanged, or otherwise disposed of within 3 years of the original contribution, describe each item in detail. For a motor vehicle, include the vehicle identification number. For a boat, include the hull identification number. For an airplane, include the aircraft identification number. Additionally, for the period of time the organization owned the property, explain how it was used. If additional space is needed, attach a statement.

Column 3. Check "Yes" if the organization's use of the charitable deduction property was related to its exempt purpose or function. Check "No" if the organization sold, exchanged, or otherwise disposed of the property without using it.

Signature

Form 8282 is not valid unless it is signed by an officer of the organization. Be sure to include the title of the person signing the form and the date the form was signed.

How To Get Tax Help

Internet

You can access the IRS website 24 hours a day, 7 days a week at *www.irs.gov/eo* to:

● Download forms, instructions, and publications;

● Order IRS products online;

● Research your tax questions online;

● Search publications online by topic or keyword;

● View Internal Revenue Bulletins (IRBs) published in the last few years; and

● Sign up to receive local and national tax news by email. To subscribe, visit *www.irs.gov/eo.*

DVD

You can order Publication 1796, IRS Tax Products DVD, and obtain:

● Current-year forms, instructions, and publications.

● Prior-year forms, instructions, and publications.

● Tax Map: an electronic research tool and finding aid.

● Tax law frequently asked questions.

● Tax topics from the IRS telephone response system.

● Fill-in, print, and save features for most tax forms.

● IRBs.

● Toll-free and email technical support.

● Two releases during the year.

Purchase the DVD from National Technical Information Service (NTIS) at *www.irs.gov/cdorders* for $30 (no handling fee) or call **1-877-CDFORMS** (1-877-233-6767) toll-free to buy the DVD for $30 (plus a $6 handling fee). Price is subject to change.

By Phone

You can order forms and publications by calling 1-800-TAX-FORM (1-800-829-3676). You can also get most forms and publications at your local IRS office. If you have questions and/or need help completing this form, please call 1-877-829-5500. This toll free telephone service is available Monday thru Friday.

Paperwork Reduction Act Notice. We ask for the information on this form to carry out the Internal Revenue laws of the United States. You are required to give us the information. We need it to ensure that you are complying with these laws and to allow us to figure and collect the right amount of tax.

You are not required to provide the information requested on a form that is subject to the Paperwork Reduction Act unless the form displays a valid OMB control number. Books or records relating to a form or its instructions must be retained as long as their contents may become material in the administration of any Internal Revenue law. Generally, tax returns and return information are confidential, as required by section 6103.

The time needed to complete this form will vary depending on individual circumstances. The estimated average time is:

Recordkeeping . . . . . 3 hr., 35 min.

Learning about the law or the form . . . . 12 min.

Preparing and sending the form to the IRS . . . . 15 min.

If you have comments concerning the accuracy of these time estimates or suggestions for making this form simpler, we would be happy to hear from you. You can write to the Internal Revenue Service, Tax Products Coordinating Committee, SE:W:CAR:MP:T:T:SP, 1111 Constitution Ave. NW, IR-6526, Washington, DC 20224. Do not send the form to this address. Instead, see *Where To File* on page 3.

Figure 37.1. *(continued)*

Preferred Object Identification Format for Art* Valued Over $50,000

Note: This format is recommended for the object identification section in your appraisal report. It is not intended to stand alone as an appraisal report.

* Art includes paintings, sculptures, watercolors, prints, drawings, ceramics, antiques, decorative arts, textiles, carpets, silver, rare manuscripts, historical memorabilia, and other similar objects.

VALUATION EFFECTIVE DATE:

FAIR MARKET VALUE: $

ARTIST: Artist (last name, first name) (nationality, dates) or Culture or Maker

DESCRIPTION: A complete description of the object, including but not limited to:
- Title or Type of Object
- Date or Period
- Medium (materials and techniques)
- Dimensions
- Signature, inscriptions or other identifying details
- Subject matter

PROVENANCE:

EXHIBITIONS:

LITERARY REFERENCES/CATALOGUE RAISONNÉ:

CONDITION:

ACQUISITION COST, DATE AND SOURCE:

APPRAISED VALUE SUPPORT:

AUCTION OR PRIVATE SALES:

PRICE For example:	SALE, LOCATION, DATE, LOT #	DESCRIPTION
$50,000	Jones Auctions, NY, NY: 06/04/09, #435	*House on a Hill*, 1990 Oil on canvas 24 x 32 inches
$65,000	Smith Gallery, Wash., DC: 5/15/09	*House by a Stream*, 1962 Oil on canvas 20 x 24 inches

Include images of your comparable sales and/or the auction catalogue pages.

March 2011

Figure 37.2. IRS Form: Preferred Object Identification Format for Art* Valued over $50,000

REASONING FOR APPRAISED VALUE:

The appraisal of each work should provide the basis or reasoning as to how the appraiser arrived at the individual appraised value. Individual comparable sales should be included. These sales should be analyzed in terms of quality, etc. and discussed as to how they relate to the subject property. The item discussion should include commentary regarding any special conditions or circumstances about the property, and a discussion of the quality or importance of the property in relation to other works of art by the same artist, and of the state of the art market at the time of valuation. Whenever possible, statements should be supported with factual evidence.

Note: It is understood that complete information will not be readily available in every case. However, the validity of the appraiser's valuation is enhanced and the IRS's appraisal review facilitated by complete and accurate information. This object identification should be accompanied by a professional quality photograph of the subject property (See photographic requirements).

March 2011

Figure 37.2.   *(continued)*

Publication 561
(Rev. February 2020)

Cat. No. 15109Q

Department
of the
Treasury

Internal
Revenue
Service

Determining the Value of Donated Property

Contents

Introduction

This publication is designed to help donors and appraisers determine the value of property (other than cash) that is given to qualified organizations. It also explains what kind of information you must have to support the charitable contribution deduction you claim on your return.

This publication does not discuss how to figure the amount of your deduction for charitable contributions or written records and substantiation required. See Pub. 526, Charitable Contributions, for this information.

Comments and suggestions. We welcome your comments about this publication and your suggestions for future editions.

You can send us comments through *IRS.gov/FormComments*. Or, you can write to: Internal Revenue Service, Tax Forms and Publications, 1111 Constitution Ave. NW, IR-6526, Washington, DC 20224.

Although we can't respond individually to each comment received, we do appreciate your feedback and will consider your comments as we revise our tax forms, instructions, and publications. We can't answer tax questions sent to the above address.

Tax questions. If you have a tax question not answered by this publication or *How To Get Tax Help* section at the end of this publication, go to the IRS Interactive Tax Assistant page at *IRS.gov/Help/ITA* where you can find topics using the search feature or by viewing the categories listed.

Getting tax forms, instructions, and publications. Visit *IRS.gov/Forms* to download current and prior-year forms, instructions, and publications.

Ordering tax forms, instructions, and publications. Go to *IRS.gov/OrderForms* to order current forms, instructions, and publications; call 800-829-3676 to order prior-year forms and instructions. Your order should arrive within 10 business days.

Useful Items
You may want to see:

Publication

❏ **526** Charitable Contributions

Get forms and other information faster and easier at:
- *IRS.gov* (English)
- *IRS.gov/Korean* (한국어)
- *IRS.gov/Spanish* (Español)
- *IRS.gov/Russian* (Русский)
- *IRS.gov/Chinese* (中文)
- *IRS.gov/Vietnamese* (TiếngViệt)

Feb 06, 2020

Figure 37.3. IRS Publication 561: Determining the Value of Donated Property

Forms (and Instructions)

❑ **8282** Donee Information Return

❑ **8283** Noncash Charitable Contributions

❑ **8283-V** Payment Voucher for Filing Fee Under Section 170(f)(13)

See *How To Get Tax Help* near the end of this publication, for information about getting these publications and forms.

What Is Fair Market Value (FMV)?

To figure how much you may deduct for property that you contribute, you must first determine its fair market value on the date of the contribution.

Fair market value. Fair market value (FMV) is the price that property would sell for on the open market. It is the price that would be agreed on between a willing buyer and a willing seller, with neither being required to act, and both having reasonable knowledge of the relevant facts. If you put a restriction on the use of property you donate, the FMV must reflect that restriction.

Example 1. If you give used clothing to the Salvation Army, the FMV would be the price that typical buyers actually pay for clothing of this age, condition, style, and use. Usually, such items are worth far less than what you paid for them.

Example 2. If you donate land and restrict its use to agricultural purposes, you must value the land at its value for agricultural purposes, even though it would have a higher FMV if it were not restricted.

Factors. In making and supporting the valuation of property, all factors affecting value are relevant and must be considered. These include:

- The cost or selling price of the item,
- Sales of comparable properties,
- Replacement cost, and
- Opinions of experts.

These factors are discussed later. Also, see *Table 1* for a summary of questions to ask as you consider each factor.

Date of contribution. Ordinarily, the date of a contribution is the date that the transfer of the property takes place.

Stock. If you deliver, without any conditions, a properly endorsed stock certificate to a qualified organization or to an agent of the organization, the date of the contribution is the date of delivery. If the certificate is mailed and received through the regular mail, it is the date of mailing. If you deliver the certificate to a bank or broker acting as your agent or to the issuing corporation or its agent, for transfer into the name of the organization, the date of the contribution is the date the stock is transferred on the books of the corporation.

Options. If you grant an option to a qualified organization to buy real property, you have

not made a charitable contribution until the organization exercises the option. The amount of the contribution is the FMV of the property on the date the option is exercised minus the exercise price.

Example. You grant an option to a local university, which is a qualified organization, to buy real property. Under the option, the university could buy the property at any time during a 2-year period for $40,000. The FMV of the property on the date the option is granted is $50,000.

In the following tax year, the university exercises the option. The FMV of the property on the date the option is exercised is $55,000. Therefore, you have made a charitable contribution of $15,000 ($55,000, the FMV, minus $40,000, the exercise price) in the tax year the option is exercised.

Determining Fair Market Value

Determining the value of donated property would be a simple matter if you could rely only on fixed formulas, rules, or methods. Usually it is not that simple. Using such formulas, etc., seldom results in an acceptable determination of FMV. There is no single formula that always applies when determining the value of property.

This is not to say that a valuation is only guesswork. You must consider all the facts and circumstances connected with the property, such as its desirability, use, and scarcity.

For example, donated furniture should not be evaluated at some fixed rate such as 15% of the cost of new replacement furniture. When the furniture is contributed, it may be out of style or in poor condition, therefore having little or no market value. On the other hand, it may be an antique, the value of which could not be determined by using any formula.

Cost or Selling Price of the Donated Property

The cost of the property to you or the actual selling price received by the qualified organization may be the best indication of its FMV. However, because conditions in the market change, the cost or selling price of property may have less weight if the property was not bought or sold reasonably close to the date of contribution.

The cost or selling price is a good indication of the property's value if:

- The purchase or sale took place close to the valuation date in an open market,
- The purchase or sale was at "arm's-length,"
- The buyer and seller knew all relevant facts,
- The buyer and seller did not have to act, and
- The market did not change between the date of purchase or sale and the valuation date.

Example. Tom Morgan, who is not a dealer in gems, bought an assortment of gems for

$5,000 from a promoter. The promoter claimed that the price was "wholesale" even though he and other dealers made similar sales at similar prices to other persons who were not dealers. The promoter said that if Tom kept the gems for more than 1 year and then gave them to charity, Tom could claim a charitable deduction of $15,000, which, according to the promoter, would be the value of the gems at the time of contribution. Tom gave the gems to a qualified charity 13 months after buying them.

The selling price for these gems had not changed from the date of purchase to the date he donated them to charity. The best evidence of FMV depends on actual transactions and not on some artificial estimate. The $5,000 charged Tom and others is, therefore, the best evidence of the maximum FMV of the gems.

Terms of the purchase or sale. The terms of the purchase or sale should be considered in determining FMV if they influenced the price. These terms include any restrictions, understandings, or covenants limiting the use or disposition of the property.

Rate of increase or decrease in value. Unless you can show that there were unusual circumstances, it is assumed that the increase or decrease in the value of your donated property from your cost has been at a reasonable rate. For time adjustments, an appraiser may consider published price indexes for information on general price trends, building costs, commodity costs, securities, and works of art sold at auction in arm's-length sales.

Example. Bill Brown bought a painting for $10,000. Thirteen months later he gave it to an art museum, claiming a charitable deduction of $15,000 on his tax return. The appraisal of the painting should include information showing that there were unusual circumstances that justify a 50% increase in value for the 13 months Bill held the property.

Arm's-length offer. An arm's-length offer to buy the property close to the valuation date may help to prove its value if the person making the offer was willing and able to complete the transaction. To rely on an offer, you should be able to show proof of the offer and the specific amount to be paid. Offers to buy property other than the donated item will help to determine value if the other property is reasonably similar to the donated property.

Sales of Comparable Properties

The sales prices of properties similar to the donated property are often important in determining the FMV. The weight to be given to each sale depends on the following.

- The degree of similarity between the property sold and the donated property.
- The time of the sale—whether it was close to the valuation date.
- The circumstances of the sale—whether it was at arm's-length with a knowledgeable buyer and seller, with neither having to act.
- The conditions of the market in which the sale was made—whether unusually inflated or deflated.

Page 2

Figure 37.3. *(continued)*

Table 1. **Factors That Affect FMV**

IF the factor you are considering is...	THEN you should ask these questions...
cost or selling price	Was the purchase or sale of the property reasonably close to the date of contribution?
	Was any increase or decrease in value, as compared to your cost, at a reasonable rate?
	Do the terms of purchase or sale limit what can be done with the property?
	Was there an arm's-length offer to buy the property close to the valuation date?
sales of comparable properties	How similar is the property sold to the property donated?
	How close is the date of sale to the valuation date?
	Was the sale at arm's-length?
	What was the condition of the market at the time of sale?
replacement cost	What would it cost to replace the donated property?
	Is there a reasonable relationship between replacement cost and FMV?
	Is the supply of the donated property more or less than the demand for it?
opinions of experts	Is the expert knowledgeable and competent?
	Is the opinion thorough and supported by facts and experience?

The comparable sales method of valuing real estate is explained, later, under *Valuation of Various Kinds of Property*.

Example 1. Mary Black, who is not a book dealer, paid a promoter $10,000 for 500 copies of a single edition of a modern translation of the Bible. The promoter had claimed that the price was considerably less than the "retail" price, and gave her a statement that the books had a total retail value of $30,000. The promoter advised her that if she kept the Bibles for more than 1 year and then gave them to a qualified organization, she could claim a charitable deduction for the "retail" price of $30,000. Thirteen months later she gave all the bibles to a church that she selected from a list provided by the promoter. At the time of her donation, wholesale dealers were selling similar quantities of bibles to the general public for $10,000.

The FMV of the bibles is $10,000, the price at which similar quantities of bibles were being sold to others at the time of the contribution.

Example 2. The facts are the same as in *Example 1*, except that the promoter gave Mary Black a second option. The promoter said that if Mary wanted a charitable deduction within 1 year of the purchase, she could buy the 500 bibles at the "retail" price of $30,000, paying only $10,000 in cash and giving a promissory note for the remaining $20,000. The principal and interest on the note would not be due for 12 years. According to the promoter, Mary could then, within 1 year of the purchase, give the bibles to a qualified organization and claim the full $30,000 retail price as a charitable contribution. She purchased the bibles under the second option and, 3 months later, gave them to a church, which will use the books for church purposes.

At the time of the gift, the promoter was selling similar lots of bibles for either $10,000 or $30,000. The difference between the two prices was solely at the discretion of the buyer. The promoter was a willing seller for $10,000. Therefore, the value of Mary's contribution of the bibles is $10,000, the amount at which similar lots of bibles could be purchased from the promoter by members of the general public.

Replacement Cost

The cost of buying, building, or manufacturing property similar to the donated item should be considered in determining FMV. However, there must be a reasonable relationship between the replacement cost and the FMV.

The replacement cost is the amount it would cost to replace the donated item on the valuation date. Often there is no relationship between the replacement cost and the FMV. If the supply of the donated property is more or less than the demand for it, the replacement cost becomes less important.

To determine the replacement cost of the donated property, find the "estimated replacement cost new." Then subtract from this figure an amount for depreciation due to the physical condition and obsolescence of the donated property. You should be able to show the relationship between the depreciated replacement cost and the FMV, as well as how you arrived at the "estimated replacement cost new."

Opinions of Experts

Generally, the weight given to an expert's opinion on matters such as the authenticity of a coin or a work of art, or the most profitable and best use of a piece of real estate, depends on the knowledge and competence of the expert and the thoroughness with which the opinion is supported by experience and facts. For an expert's opinion to deserve much weight, the facts must support the opinion. For additional information, see *Appraisals*, later.

Problems in Determining Fair Market Value

There are a number of problems in determining the FMV of donated property.

Unusual Market Conditions

The sale price of the property itself in an arm's-length transaction in an open market is often the best evidence of its value. When you rely on sales of comparable property, the sales must have been made in an open market. If those sales were made in a market that was artificially supported or stimulated so as not to be truly representative, the prices at which the sales were made will not indicate the FMV.

For example, liquidation sale prices usually do not indicate the FMV. Also, sales of stock under unusual circumstances, such as sales of small lots, forced sales, and sales in a restricted market, may not represent the FMV.

Selection of Comparable Sales

Using sales of comparable property is an important method for determining the FMV of donated property. However, the amount of weight given to a sale depends on the degree of similarity between the comparable and the donated properties. The degree of similarity must be close enough so that this selling price would have been given consideration by reasonably well-informed buyers or sellers of the property.

Example. You give a rare, old book to your former college. The book is a third edition and is in poor condition because of a missing back cover. You discover that there was a sale for $300, near the valuation date, of a first edition of the book that was in good condition. Although the contents are the same, the books are not at all similar because of the different editions and their physical condition. Little consideration would be given to the selling price of the $300 property by knowledgeable buyers or sellers.

Future Events

You may not consider unexpected events happening after your donation of property in making the valuation. You may consider only the facts known at the time of the gift, and those that could be reasonably expected at the time of the gift.

Example. You give farmland to a qualified charity. The transfer provides that your mother will have the right to all income and full use of the property for her life. Even though your mother dies 1 week after the transfer, the value of the property on the date it is given is its present value, subject to the life interest as estimated from actuarial tables. You may not take a higher deduction because the charity received full use and possession of the land only 1 week after the transfer.

Using Past Events to Predict the Future

A common error is to rely too much on past events that do not fairly reflect the probable future earnings and FMV.

Figure 37.3. *(continued)*

Example. You give all your rights in a successful patent to your favorite charity. Your records show that before the valuation date there were three stages in the patent's history of earnings. First, there was rapid growth in earnings when the invention was introduced. Then, there was a period of high earnings when the invention was being exploited. Finally, there was a decline in earnings when competing inventions were introduced. The entire history of earnings may be relevant in estimating the future earnings. However, the appraiser must not rely too much on the stage of rapid growth in earnings or of high earnings. The market conditions at those times do not represent the condition of the market at the valuation date. What is most significant is the trend of decline in earnings up to the valuation date. For more information about donations of patents, see *Patents,* later.

Valuation of Various Kinds of Property

This section contains information on determining the FMV of ordinary kinds of donated property. For information on appraisals, see *Appraisals,* later.

Household Goods

The FMV of used household goods, such as furniture, appliances, and linens, is usually much lower than the price paid when new. Such used property may have little or no market value because of its worn condition. It may be out of style or no longer useful.

You cannot take a deduction for household goods unless they are in good used condition or better. A household good that is not in good used condition or better for which you take a deduction of more than $500 requires a qualified appraisal and Form 8283, Section B. See *Deduction over $500 for certain clothing or household items,* later.

If the property is valuable because it is old or unique, see the discussion under *Paintings, Antiques, and Other Objects of Art*.

Used Clothing

Used clothing and other personal items are usually worth far less than the price you paid for them. Valuation of items of clothing does not lend itself to fixed formulas or methods.

The price that buyers of used items actually pay in used clothing stores, such as consignment or thrift shops, is an indication of the value.

You cannot take a deduction for clothing unless it is in good used condition or better. An item of clothing that is not in good used condition or better for which you take a deduction of more than $500 requires a qualified appraisal and Form 8283, Section B. See *Deduction over $500 for certain clothing or household items,* later.

Jewelry and Gems

Jewelry and gems are of such a specialized nature that it is almost always necessary to get an appraisal by a specialized jewelry appraiser. The appraisal should describe, among other things, the style of the jewelry, the cut and setting of the gem, and whether it is now in fashion. If not in fashion, the possibility of having the property redesigned, recut, or reset should be reported in the appraisal. The stone's coloring, weight, cut, brilliance, and flaws should be reported and analyzed. Sentimental personal value has no effect on FMV. But if the jewelry was owned by a famous person, its value might increase.

Paintings, Antiques, and Other Objects of Art

Your deduction for contributions of paintings, antiques, and other objects of art, should be supported by a written appraisal from a qualified and reputable source, unless the deduction is $5,000 or less. Examples of information that should be included in appraisals of art objects—paintings in particular—are found later under *Qualified Appraisal*.

Art valued at $20,000 or more. If you claim a deduction of $20,000 or more for donations of art, you must attach a complete copy of the signed appraisal to your return. For individual objects valued at $20,000 or more, a photograph of a size and quality fully showing the object, preferably an 8 x 10 inch color photograph or a high-resolution digital image, must be provided upon request.

Art valued at $50,000 or more. If you donate an item of art that has been appraised at $50,000 or more, you can request a Statement of Value for that item from the IRS. You must request the statement before filing the tax return that reports the donation. Your request must include the following.

- A copy of a qualified appraisal of the item. See *Qualified Appraisal*, later.
- A user fee of $6,500 for one to three items ($7,500 for requests received after February 1, 2020) and $300 for each additional item ($400 for requests received after February 1, 2020) paid through *Pay.gov*. A payment confirmation will be provided to you through the *Pay.gov* portal and you should submit the payment confirmation with your Statement of Value request.
- A completed Form 8283, Section B.
- The location of the IRS territory that has examination responsibility for your return.

If your request lacks essential information, you will be notified and given 30 days to provide the missing information.

Send your request to:

Internal Revenue Service/Art Appraisal Services
1111 Constitution Ave., Suite 700
C:AP:SO:ART
Washington, DC 20224-0002
ATTN: AAS

Refunds. You can withdraw your request for a Statement of Value at any time before it is issued. However, the IRS will not refund the user fee if you do.

If the IRS declines to issue a Statement of Value in the interest of efficient tax administration, the IRS will refund the user fee.

Authenticity. The authenticity of the donated art must be determined by the appraiser.

Physical condition. Important items in the valuation of antiques and art are physical condition and extent of restoration. These have a significant effect on the value and must be fully reported in an appraisal. An antique in damaged condition, or lacking the "original brasses," may be worth much less than a similar piece in excellent condition.

Art appraisers. More weight will usually be given to an appraisal prepared by an individual specializing in the kind and price range of the art being appraised. Certain art dealers or appraisers specialize, for example, in old masters, modern art, bronze sculpture, etc. Their opinions on the authenticity and desirability of such art would usually be given more weight than the opinions of more generalized art dealers or appraisers. They can report more recent comparable sales to support their opinion.

To identify and locate experts on unique, specialized items or collections, you may wish to use the current Official Museum Directory of the American Association of Museums. It lists museums both by state and by category.

To help you locate a qualified appraiser for your donation, you may wish to search on the Internet. You may also wish to ask an art historian at a nearby college or the director or curator of a local museum. You may also contact associations of dealers for guidance.

Collections

Since many kinds of hobby collections may be the subject of a charitable donation, it is not possible to discuss all of the possible collectibles in this publication. Most common are rare books, autographs, sports memorabilia, dolls, manuscripts, stamps, coins, guns, phonograph records, and natural history items. Many of the elements of valuation that apply to paintings and other objects of art, discussed earlier, also apply to miscellaneous collections.

Reference material. Publications available to help you determine the value of many kinds of collections include catalogs, dealers' price lists, and specialized hobby periodicals. When using one of these price guides, you must use the current edition at the date of contribution. However, these sources are not always reliable indicators of FMV and should be supported by other evidence.

For example, a dealer may sell an item for much less than is shown on a price list, particularly after the item has remained unsold for a long time. The price an item sold for in an auction may have been the result of a rigged sale or a mere bidding duel. The appraiser must analyze the reference material, and recognize and make adjustments for misleading entries. If you

Publication 561 (February 2020)

Figure 37.3. *(continued)*

are donating a valuable collection, you should get an appraisal. If your donation appears to be of little value, you may be able to make a satisfactory valuation using reference materials available at a state, city, college, or museum library.

Stamp collections. Most libraries have catalogs or other books that report the publisher's estimate of values. Generally, two price levels are shown for each stamp: the price postmarked and the price not postmarked. Stamp dealers generally know the value of their merchandise and are able to prepare satisfactory appraisals of valuable collections.

Coin collections. Many catalogs and other reference materials show the writer's or publisher's opinion of the value of coins on or near the date of the publication. Like many other collectors' items, the value of a coin depends on the demand for it, its age, and its rarity. Another important factor is the coin's condition. For example, there is a great difference in the value of a coin that is in mint condition and a similar coin that is only in good condition.

Catalogs usually establish a category for coins, based on their physical condition—mint or uncirculated, extremely fine, very fine, fine, very good, good, fair, or poor—with a different valuation for each category.

Books. The value of books is usually determined by selecting comparable sales and adjusting the prices according to the differences between the comparable sales and the item being evaluated. This is difficult to do and, except for a collection of little value, should be done by a specialized appraiser. Within the general category of literary property, there are dealers who specialize in certain areas, such as Americana, foreign imports, bibles, and scientific books.

Modest value of collection. If the collection you are donating is of modest value, not requiring a written appraisal, the following information may help you in determining the FMV.

A book that is very old, or very rare, is not necessarily valuable. There are many books that are very old or rare, but that have little or no market value.

Condition of book. The condition of a book may have a great influence on its value. Collectors are interested in items that are in fine, or at least good, condition. When a book has a missing page, a loose binding, tears, stains, or is otherwise in poor condition, its value is greatly lowered.

Other factors. Some other factors in the valuation of a book are the kind of binding (leather, cloth, paper), page edges, and illustrations (drawings and photographs). Collectors usually want first editions of books. However, because of changes or additions, other editions are sometimes worth as much as, or more than, the first edition.

Manuscripts, autographs, diaries, and similar items. When these items are handwritten, or at least signed by famous people, they are often in demand and are valuable. The writings of unknowns also may be of value if they are of unusual historical or literary importance. Deter-

mining the value of such material is difficult. For example, there may be a great difference in value between two diaries that were kept by a famous person—one kept during childhood and the other during a later period in his or her life. The appraiser determines a value in these cases by applying knowledge and judgment to such factors as comparable sales and conditions.

Signatures. Signatures, or sets of signatures, that were cut from letters or other papers usually have little or no value. But complete sets of the signatures of U.S. presidents are in demand.

Cars, Boats, and Aircraft

If you donate a car, a boat, or an aircraft to a charitable organization, its FMV must be determined.

Certain commercial firms and trade organizations publish monthly or seasonal guides for different regions of the country, containing complete dealer sale prices or dealer average prices for recent model years. Prices are reported for each make, model, and year. These guides also provide estimates for adjusting for unusual equipment, unusual mileage, and physical condition. The prices are not "official," and these publications are not considered an appraisal of any specific donated property. But they do provide clues for making an appraisal and suggest relative prices for comparison with current sales and offerings in your area.

These publications are sometimes available from public libraries or at a bank, credit union, or finance company. You can also find pricing information about used cars on the Internet.

An acceptable measure of the FMV of a donated car, boat, or airplane is an amount not in excess of the price listed in a used vehicle pricing guide for a private party sale, not the dealer retail value, of a similar vehicle. However, the FMV may be less than that amount if the vehicle has engine trouble, body damage, high mileage, or any type of excessive wear. The FMV of a donated vehicle is the same as the price listed in a used vehicle pricing guide for a private party sale only if the guide lists a sales price for a vehicle that is the same make, model, and year, sold in the same area, in the same condition, with the same or similar options or accessories, and with the same or similar warranties as the donated vehicle.

Example. You donate a used car in poor condition to a local high school for use by students studying car repair. A used car guide shows the dealer retail value for this type of car in poor condition is $1,600. However, the guide shows the price for a private party sale of the car is only $750. The FMV of the car is considered to be no more than $750.

Boats. Except for inexpensive small boats, the valuation of boats should be based on an appraisal by a marine surveyor because the physical condition is so critical to the value.

More information. Your deduction for a donated car, boat, or airplane generally is limited to

the gross proceeds from its sale by the qualified organization. This rule applies if the claimed value of the donated vehicle is more than $500. In certain cases, you can deduct the vehicle's FMV. For details, see Pub. 526.

Inventory

If you donate any inventory item to a charitable organization, the amount of your deductible contribution generally is the FMV of the item, minus any gain you would have realized if you had sold the item at its FMV on the date of the gift. For more information, see Pub. 526.

Patents

To determine the FMV of a patent, you must take into account, among other factors:
- Whether the patented technology has been made obsolete by other technology;
- Any restrictions on the donee's use of, or ability to transfer, the patented technology; and
- The length of time remaining before the patent expires.

However, your deduction for a donation of a patent or other intellectual property is its FMV, minus any gain you would have realized if you had sold the property at its FMV on the date of the gift. Generally, this means your deduction is the lesser of the property's FMV or its basis. For details, see Pub. 526.

Stocks and Bonds

The value of stocks and bonds is the FMV of a share or bond on the valuation date. See *Date of contribution,* earlier, under *What Is Fair Market Value (FMV)?*.

Selling prices on valuation date. If there is an active market for the contributed stocks or bonds on a stock exchange, in an over-the-counter market, or elsewhere, the FMV of each share or bond is the average price between the highest and lowest quoted selling prices on the valuation date. For example, if the highest selling price for a share was $11 and the lowest $9, the average price is $10. You get the average price by adding $11 and $9 and dividing the sum by 2.

No sales on valuation date. If there were no sales on the valuation date, but there were sales within a reasonable period before and after the valuation date, you determine FMV by taking the average price between the highest and lowest sales prices on the nearest date before and on the nearest date after the valuation date. Then you weight these averages in inverse order by the respective number of trading days between the selling dates and the valuation date.

Example. On the day you gave stock to a qualified organization, there were no sales of the stock. Sales of the stock nearest the valuation date took place two trading days before the valuation date at an average selling price of $10 and three trading days after the valuation date at an average selling price of $15. The FMV on the valuation date was $12, figured as follows.

Figure 37.3. *(continued)*

$$[(3 \times \$10) + (2 \times \$15)] \div 5 = \$12$$

Listings on more than one stock exchange. Stocks or bonds listed on more than one stock exchange are valued based on the prices of the exchange on which they are principally dealt. This applies if these prices are published in a generally available listing or publication of general circulation. If this is not applicable, and the stocks or bonds are reported on a composite listing of combined exchanges in a publication of general circulation, use the composite list. See also *Unavailable prices or closely held corporation.*

Bid and asked prices on valuation date. If there were no sales within a reasonable period before and after the valuation date, the FMV is the average price between the bona fide bid and asked prices on the valuation date.

Example. Although there were no sales of Blue Corporation stock on the valuation date, bona fide bid and asked prices were available on that date of $14 and $16, respectively. The FMV is $15, the average price between the bid and asked prices.

No prices on valuation date. If there were no prices available on the valuation date, you determine FMV by taking the average prices between the bona fide bid and asked prices on the closest trading date before and after the valuation date. Both dates must be within a reasonable period. Then you weight these averages in inverse order by the respective number of trading days between the bid and asked dates and the valuation date.

Example. On the day you gave stock to a qualified organization, no prices were available. Bona fide bid and asked prices 3 days before the valuation date were $10 and 2 days after the valuation date were $15. The FMV on the valuation date is $13, figured as follows:

$$[(2 \times \$10) + (3 \times \$15)] \div 5 = \$13$$

Prices only before or after valuation date, but not both. If no selling prices or bona fide bid and asked prices are available on a date within a reasonable period before the valuation date, but are available on a date within a reasonable period after the valuation date, or vice versa, then the average price between the highest and lowest of such available prices may be treated as the value.

Large blocks of stock. When a large block of stock is put on the market, it may lower the selling price of the stock if the supply is greater than the demand. On the other hand, market forces may exist that will afford higher prices for large blocks of stock. Because of the many factors to be considered, determining the value of large blocks of stock usually requires the help of experts specializing in underwriting large quantities of securities or in trading in the securities of the industry of which the particular company is a part.

Unavailable prices or closely held corporation. If selling prices or bid and asked prices are not available, or if securities of a closely held corporation are involved, determine the FMV by considering the following factors.

- For bonds, the soundness of the security, the interest yield, the date of maturity, and other relevant factors.
- For shares of stock, the company's net worth, prospective earning power and dividend-paying capacity, and other relevant factors.

Other factors. Other relevant factors include:

- The nature and history of the business, especially its recent history;
- The goodwill of the business;
- The economic outlook in the particular industry;
- The company's position in the industry, its competitors, and its management; and
- The value of securities of corporations engaged in the same or similar business.

For preferred stock, the most important factors are its yield, dividend coverage, and protection of its liquidation preference.

You should keep complete financial and other information on which the valuation is based. This includes copies of reports of examinations of the company made by accountants, engineers, or any technical experts on or close to the valuation date.

Restricted securities. Some classes of stock cannot be traded publicly because of restrictions imposed by the Securities and Exchange Commission, or by the corporate charter or a trust agreement. These restricted securities usually trade at a discount in relation to freely traded securities.

To arrive at the FMV of restricted securities, factors that you must consider include the resale provisions found in the restriction agreements, the relative negotiating strengths of the buyer and seller, and the market experience of freely traded securities of the same class as the restricted securities.

Real Estate

Because each piece of real estate is unique and its valuation is complicated, a detailed appraisal by a professional appraiser is necessary.

The appraiser must be thoroughly trained in the application of appraisal principles and theory. In some instances the opinions of equally qualified appraisers may carry unequal weight, such as when one appraiser has a better knowledge of local conditions.

The appraisal report must contain a complete description of the property, such as street address, legal description, and lot and block number, as well as physical features, condition, and dimensions. The use to which the property is put, zoning and permitted uses, and its potential use for other higher and better uses are also relevant.

In general, there are three main approaches to the valuation of real estate. An appraisal may require the combined use of two or three methods rather than one method only.

1. Comparable Sales

The comparable sales method compares the donated property with several similar properties that have been sold. The selling prices, after adjustments for differences in date of sale, size, condition, and location, would then indicate the estimated FMV of the donated property.

If the comparable sales method is used to determine the value of unimproved real property (land without significant buildings, structures, or any other improvements that add to its value), the appraiser should consider the following factors when comparing the potential comparable property and the donated property:

- Location, size, and zoning or use restrictions;
- Accessibility and road frontage, and available utilities and water rights;
- Riparian rights (right of access to and use of the water by owners of land on the bank of a river) and existing easements, rights-of-way, leases, etc.;
- Soil characteristics, vegetative cover, and status of mineral rights; and
- Other factors affecting value.

For each comparable sale, the appraisal must include the names of the buyer and seller, the deed book and page number, the date of sale and selling price, a property description, the amount and terms of mortgages, property surveys, the assessed value, the tax rate, and the assessor's appraised FMV.

The comparable selling prices must be adjusted to account for differences between the sale property and the donated property. Because differences of opinion may arise between appraisers as to the degree of comparability and the amount of the adjustment considered necessary for comparison purposes, an appraiser should document each item of adjustment.

Only comparable sales having the least adjustments in terms of items and/or total dollar adjustments should be considered as comparable to the donated property.

2. Capitalization of Income

This method capitalizes the net income from the property at a rate that represents a fair return on the particular investment at the particular time, considering the risks involved. The key elements are the determination of the income to be capitalized and the rate of capitalization.

3. Replacement Cost New or Reproduction Cost Minus Observed Depreciation

This method, used alone, usually does not result in a determination of FMV. Instead, it generally tends to set the upper limit of value, particularly in periods of rising costs, because it is reasonable to assume that an informed buyer will not pay more for the real estate than it would cost to reproduce a similar property. Of course, this reasoning does not apply if a similar property cannot be created because of location, unusual construction, or some other

Publication 561 (February 2020)

Figure 37.3. *(continued)*

reason. Generally, this method serves to support the value determined from other methods. When the replacement cost method is applied to improved realty, the land and improvements are valued separately.

The replacement cost of a building is figured by considering the materials, the quality of workmanship, and the number of square feet or cubic feet in the building. This cost represents the total cost of labor and material, overhead, and profit. After the replacement cost has been figured, consideration must be given to the following factors:

- Physical deterioration—the wear and tear on the building itself;
- Functional obsolescence—usually in older buildings with, for example, inadequate lighting, plumbing, or heating, small rooms, or a poor floor plan; and
- Economic obsolescence—outside forces causing the whole area to become less desirable.

Interest in a Business

The FMV of any interest in a business, whether a sole proprietorship or a partnership, is the amount that a willing buyer would pay for the interest to a willing seller after consideration of all relevant factors. The relevant factors to be considered in valuing the business are:

- The FMV of the assets of the business;
- The demonstrated earnings capacity of the business, based on a review of past and current earnings; and
- The other factors used in evaluating corporate stock, if they apply.

The value of the goodwill of the business should also be taken into consideration. You should keep complete financial and other information on which you base the valuation. This includes copies of reports of examinations of the business made by accountants, engineers, or any technical experts on or close to the valuation date.

Annuities, Interests for Life or Terms of Years, Remainders, and Reversions

The value of these kinds of property is their present value, except in the case of annuities under contracts issued by companies regularly engaged in their sale. The valuation of these commercial annuity contracts and of insurance policies is discussed later under *Certain Life Insurance and Annuity Contracts*.

To determine present value, you must know the applicable interest rate and use actuarial tables.

Interest rate. The applicable interest rate varies. It is announced monthly in a news release and published in the Internal Revenue Bulletin as a Revenue Ruling. The interest rate to use is under the heading "Rate Under Section 7520" for a given month and year. You can call the IRS office at 1-800-829-1040 to obtain this rate.

Figure 37.3. *(continued)*

Actuarial tables. You need to refer to actuarial tables to determine a qualified interest in the form of an annuity, any interest for life or a term of years, or any remainder interest to a charitable organization.

Use the valuation tables set forth in IRS Publications 1457, Actuarial Values (Book Aleph), and 1458, Actuarial Values (Book Beth). Both of these publications provide tables containing actuarial factors to be used in determining the present value of an annuity, an interest for life or for a term of years, or a remainder or reversionary interest. For qualified charitable transfers, you can use the factor for the month in which you made the contribution or for either of the 2 months preceding that month.

Pub. 1457 also contains actuarial factors for computing the value of a remainder interest in a charitable remainder annuity trust and a pooled income fund. Pub. 1458 contains the factors for valuing the remainder interest in a charitable remainder unitrust. You can download Publications 1457 and 1458 from *IRS.gov*. Tables containing actuarial factors for transfers to pooled income funds may also be found in Income Tax Regulation 1.642(c)-6(e)(6), transfers to charitable remainder unitrusts in Regulations section 1.664-4(e), and other transfers in Regulations section 20.2031-7(d)(6).

Special factors. If you need a special factor for an actual transaction, you can request a letter ruling. Be sure to include the date of birth of each person the duration of whose life may affect the value of the interest. Also include copies of the relevant instruments. IRS charges a user fee for providing special factors.

For more information about requesting a ruling, see Revenue Procedure 2020-1 (or annual update).

For information on the circumstances under which a charitable deduction may be allowed for the donation of a partial interest in property not in trust, see *Partial Interest in Property Not in Trust*, later.

Certain Life Insurance and Annuity Contracts

The value of an annuity contract or a life insurance policy issued by a company regularly engaged in the sale of such contracts or policies is the amount that company would charge for a comparable contract.

But if the donee of a life insurance policy may reasonably be expected to cash the policy rather than hold it as an investment, then the FMV is the cash surrender value rather than the replacement cost.

If an annuity is payable under a combination annuity contract and life insurance policy (for example, a retirement income policy with a death benefit) and there was no insurance element when it was transferred to the charity, the policy is treated as an annuity contract.

Partial Interest in Property Not in Trust

Generally, no deduction is allowed for a charitable contribution, not made in trust, of less than

your entire interest in property. However, this does not apply to a transfer of less than your entire interest if it is a transfer of:

- A remainder interest in your personal residence or farm,
- An undivided part of your entire interest in property, or
- A qualified conservation contribution.

Remainder Interest in Real Property

The amount of the deduction for a donation of a remainder interest in real property is the FMV of the remainder interest at the time of the contribution. To determine this value, you must know the FMV of the property on the date of the contribution. Multiply this value by the appropriate factor. Pubs. 1457 and 1458 contain these factors.

You must make an adjustment for depreciation or depletion using the factors shown in Pub. 1459, Actuarial Values (Book Gimel). You can use the factors for the month in which you made the contribution or for either of the two months preceding that month. See the earlier discussion on *Annuities, Interests for Life or Terms of Years, Remainders, and Reversions*. You can download Pub. 1459 from *IRS.gov*.

For this purpose, the term "depreciable property" means any property subject to wear and tear or obsolescence, even if not used in a trade or business or for the production of income.

If the remainder interest includes both depreciable and nondepreciable property, for example a house and land, the FMV must be allocated between each kind of property at the time of the contribution. This rule also applies to a gift of a remainder interest that includes property that is part depletable and part not depletable. Take into account depreciation or depletion only for the property that is subject to depreciation or depletion.

For more information, see section 1.170A-12 of the Income Tax Regulations.

Undivided Part of Your Entire Interest

A contribution of an undivided part of your entire interest in property must consist of a part of each and every substantial interest or right you own in the property. It must extend over the entire term of your interest in the property. For example, you are entitled to the income from certain property for your life (life estate) and you contribute 20% of that life estate to a qualified organization. You can claim a deduction for the contribution if you do not have any other interest in the property. To figure the value of a contribution involving a partial interest, see Pub. 1457.

If the only interest you own in real property is a remainder interest and you transfer part of that interest to a qualified organization, see the previous discussion on valuation of a remainder interest in real property.

Qualified Conservation Contribution

A qualified conservation contribution is a contribution of a qualified real property interest to a qualified organization to be used only for conservation purposes.

Qualified organization. For purposes of a qualified conservation contribution, a qualified organization is:

- A governmental unit;
- A publicly supported charitable, religious, scientific, literary, educational, etc., organization; or
- An organization that is controlled by, and operated for the exclusive benefit of, a governmental unit or a publicly supported charity.

The organization also must have a commitment to protect the conservation purposes of the donation and must have the resources to enforce the restrictions.

Conservation purposes. Your contribution must be made only for one of the following conservation purposes.

- Preserving land areas for outdoor recreation by, or for the education of, the general public.
- Protecting a relatively natural habitat of fish, wildlife, or plants, or a similar ecosystem.
- Preserving open space, including farmland and forest land, if it yields a significant public benefit. It must be either for the scenic enjoyment of the general public or under a clearly defined federal, state, or local governmental conservation policy.
- Preserving an historically important land area or a certified historic structure. There must be some visual public access to the property. Factors used in determining the type and amount of public access required include the historical significance of the property, the remoteness or accessibility of the site, and the extent to which intrusions on the privacy of individuals living on the property would be unreasonable.

Building in registered historic district. A contribution of a qualified real property interest that is an easement or other restriction on the exterior of a building in a registered historic district is deductible only if it meets all of the following three conditions.

1. The restriction must preserve the entire exterior of the building and must prohibit any change to the exterior of the building that is inconsistent with its historical character.

2. You and the organization receiving the contribution must enter into a written agreement certifying, that the organization is a qualified organization and that it has the resources and commitment to maintain the property as donated.

3. If you make the contribution, you must include with your return:

    a. A qualified appraisal,

    b. Photographs of the building's entire exterior, and

    c. A description of all restrictions on development of the building, such as zoning laws and restrictive covenants.

If you claim a deduction of more than $10,000, your deduction will not be allowed unless you pay a $500 filing fee. See Form 8283-V, Payment Voucher for Filing Fee Under Section 170(f)(13), and its instructions.

Qualified real property interest. This is any of the following interests in real property.

1. Your entire interest in real estate other than a mineral interest (subsurface oil, gas, or other minerals, and the right of access to these minerals).

2. A remainder interest.

3. A restriction (granted in perpetuity) on the use that may be made of the real property.

Valuation. A qualified real property interest described in (1) should be valued in a manner that is consistent with the type of interest transferred. If you transferred all the interest in the property, the FMV of the property is the amount of the contribution. If you do not transfer the mineral interest, the FMV of the surface rights in the property is the amount of the contribution.

If you owned only a remainder interest or an income interest (life estate), see *Undivided Part of Your Entire Interest*, earlier. If you owned the entire property but transferred only a remainder interest (item (2)), see *Remainder Interest in Real Property*, earlier.

In determining the value of restrictions, you should take into account the selling price in arm's-length transactions of other properties that have comparable restrictions. If there are no comparable sales, the restrictions are valued indirectly as the difference between the FMVs of the property involved before and after the grant of the restriction.

The FMV of the property before contribution of the restriction should take into account not only current use but the likelihood that the property, without the restriction, would be developed. You should also consider any zoning, conservation, or historical preservation laws that would restrict development. Granting an easement may increase, rather than reduce, the value of property, and in such a situation no deduction would be allowed.

Example. You own 10 acres of farmland. Similar land in the area has an FMV of $2,000 an acre. However, land in the general area that is restricted solely to farm use has an FMV of $1,500 an acre. Your county wants to preserve open space and prevent further development in your area.

You grant to the county an enforceable open space easement in perpetuity on 8 of the 10 acres, restricting its use to farmland. The value of this easement is $4,000, determined as follows:

FMV of the property before granting easement:		
$2,000 × 10 acres		$20,000
FMV of the property after granting easement:		
$1,500 × 8 acres	$12,000	
$2,000 × 2 acres	4,000	16,000
Value of easement		$4,000

If you later transfer in fee your remaining interest in the 8 acres to another qualified organization, the FMV of your remaining interest is the FMV of the 8 acres reduced by the FMV of the easement granted to the first organization.

More information. For more information about qualified conservation contributions, see Pub. 526.

Appraisals

Appraisals are not necessary for items of property for which you claim a deduction of $5,000 or less. (There is one exception, described next, for certain clothing and household items.) However, you generally will need an appraisal for donated property for which you claim a deduction of more than $5,000. There are exceptions. See *Deductions of More Than $5,000*, later.

The weight given an appraisal depends on the completeness of the report, the qualifications of the appraiser, and the appraiser's demonstrated knowledge of the donated property. An appraisal must give all the facts on which to base an intelligent judgment of the value of the property.

The appraisal will not be given much weight if:

- All the factors that apply are not considered,
- The opinion is not supported with facts, such as purchase price and comparable sales, or
- The opinion is not consistent with known facts.

The appraiser's opinion is never more valid than the facts on which it is based; without these facts it is simply a guess.

The opinion of a person claiming to be an expert is not binding on the Internal Revenue Service. All facts associated with the donation must be considered.

Deduction over $500 for certain clothing or household items. You must include with your return a qualified appraisal prepared by a qualified appraiser of any single item of clothing or any household item that is not in good used condition or better, and for which you deduct more than $500. Attach the appraisal and Form 8283, Section B, Noncash Charitable Contributions, to your return. See *Household Goods* and *Used Clothing*, earlier.

Cost of appraisals. You may not take a charitable contribution deduction for fees you pay for appraisals of your donated property.

Figure 37.3. *(continued)*

Deductions of More Than $5,000

Generally, if the claimed deduction for an item or group of similar items of donated property is more than $5,000, you must get a qualified appraisal signed and dated by a qualified appraiser and you must attach Section B of Form 8283 to your tax return. There are exceptions, discussed later. You should keep the appraiser's report with your written records. Records are discussed in Pub. 526.

The phrase "similar items" means property of the same generic category or type (whether or not donated to the same donee), such as stamp collections, coin collections, lithographs, paintings, photographs, books, nonpublicly traded stock, nonpublicly traded securities other than nonpublicly traded stock, land, buildings, clothing, jewelry, furniture, electronic equipment, household appliances, toys, everyday kitchenware, china, crystal, or silver. For example, if you give books to three schools and you deduct $2,000, $2,500, and $900, respectively, your claimed deduction is more than $5,000 for these books. You must get a qualified appraisal of the books and for each school you must attach a fully completed Form 8283, Section B, to your tax return.

Exceptions. You do not need an appraisal if the property is:

- Nonpublicly traded stock of $10,000 or less;
- A vehicle for which you obtained a contemporaneous written acknowledgement (including a car, boat, or airplane) for which your deduction is limited to the gross proceeds from its sale;
- Qualified intellectual property, such as a patent;
- Certain publicly traded securities for which market quotations are readily available;
- Inventory and other property donated by a corporation that are "qualified contributions" for the care of the ill, the needy, or infants, within the meaning of section 170(e)(3)(A) of the Internal Revenue Code; or
- Stock in trade, inventory, or property held primarily for sale to customers in the ordinary course of your trade or business.

Although an appraisal is not required for the types of property just listed, you must provide certain information about a donation of any of these types of property on Form 8283.

Publicly traded securities. Even if your claimed deduction is more than $5,000, neither a qualified appraisal nor Section B of Form 8283 is required for publicly traded securities that are:

- Listed on a stock exchange in which quotations are published on a daily basis,
- Regularly traded in a national or regional over-the-counter market for which published quotations are available, or
- Shares of an open-end investment company (mutual fund) for which quotations are published on a daily basis in a newspaper of general circulation throughout the United States.

Publicly traded securities that meet these requirements must be reported on Form 8283, Section A.

A qualified appraisal is not required, but the applicable parts of Form 8283, Section B, must be completed, for an issue of a security that does not meet the requirements just listed but does meet these requirements:

1. The issue is regularly traded during the computation period (defined later) in a market for which there is an "interdealer quotation system" (defined later),

2. The issuer or agent computes the "average trading price" (defined later) for the same issue for the computation period,

3. The average trading price and total volume of the issue during the computation period are published in a newspaper of general circulation throughout the United States, not later than the last day of the month following the end of the calendar quarter in which the computation period ends,

4. The issuer or agent keeps books and records that list for each transaction during the computation period the date of settlement of the transaction, the name and address of the broker or dealer making the market in which the transaction occurred, and the trading price and volume, and

5. The issuer or agent permits the Internal Revenue Service to review the books and records described in item (4) with respect to transactions during the computation period upon receiving reasonable notice.

An interdealer quotation system is any system of general circulation to brokers and dealers that regularly disseminates quotations of obligations by two or more identified brokers or dealers who are not related to either the issuer or agent who computes the average trading price of the security. A quotation sheet prepared and distributed by a broker or dealer in the regular course of business and containing only quotations of that broker or dealer is not an interdealer quotation system.

The average trading price is the average price of all transactions (weighted by volume), other than original issue or redemption transactions, conducted through a United States office of a broker or dealer who maintains a market in the issue of the security during the computation period. Bid and asked quotations are not taken into account.

The computation period is weekly during October through December and monthly during January through September. The weekly computation periods during October through December begin with the first Monday in October and end with the first Sunday following the last Monday in December.

Nonpublicly traded stock. If you contribute nonpublicly traded stock, for which you claim a deduction of $10,000 or less, a qualified appraisal is not required. However, you must attach Form 8283 to your tax return, with Section B, Parts I and IV, completed.

Deductions of More Than $500,000

If you claim a deduction of more than $500,000 for a donation of property, you must attach a qualified appraisal of the property to your return. This does not apply to contributions of cash, inventory, publicly traded stock, or intellectual property.

If you do not attach the appraisal, you cannot deduct your contribution, unless your failure to attach the appraisal is due to reasonable cause and not to willful neglect.

Qualified Appraisal

Generally, if the claimed deduction for an item or group of similar items of donated property is more than $5,000, you must get a qualified appraisal signed and dated by a qualified appraiser. You must also complete Form 8283, Section B, and attach it to your tax return. See *Deductions of More Than $5,000*, earlier.

A qualified appraisal is an appraisal document that:

- Is made, signed, and dated by a qualified appraiser (defined later) in accordance with generally accepted appraisal standards;
- Meets the relevant requirements of Regulations section 1.170A-17(a);
- Is dated no earlier than 60 days before the date of the contribution and no later than the date of the contribution. For an appraisal report dated on or after the date of the contribution, the valuation effective date must be the date of the contribution made not earlier than 60 days before the date of contribution of the appraised property, and
- Does not involve a prohibited appraisal fee.

You must receive the qualified appraisal before the due date, including extensions, of the return on which a charitable contribution deduction is first claimed for the donated property. If the deduction is first claimed on an amended return, the qualified appraisal must be received before the date on which the amended return is filed.

Form 8283, Section B, must be attached to your tax return. Generally, you do not need to attach the qualified appraisal itself, but you should keep a copy as long as it may be relevant under the tax law. There are four exceptions.

- If you claim a deduction of $20,000 or more for donations of art, you must attach a complete copy of the appraisal. See *Paintings, Antiques, and Other Objects of Art*, earlier.
- If you claim a deduction of more than $500,000 for a donation of property, you must attach the appraisal. See *Deductions of More Than $500,000*, earlier.
- If you claim a deduction of more than $500 for an article of clothing, or a household item, that is not in good used condition or better, you must attach the appraisal and Section B of Form 8283 to your return. See

Figure 37.3. *(continued)*

Deduction over $500 for certain clothing or household items, earlier.

- If you claim a deduction for an easement or other restriction on the exterior of a building in a historic district, you must attach the appraisal. See *Building in registered historic district*, earlier.

Prohibited appraisal fee. Generally, no part of the fee arrangement for a qualified appraisal can be based on a percentage of the appraised value of the property. If a fee arrangement is based on what is allowed as a deduction, after Internal Revenue Service examination or otherwise, it is treated as a fee based on a percentage of appraised value. However, appraisals are not disqualified when an otherwise prohibited fee is paid to a generally recognized association that regulates appraisers if:

- The association is not organized for profit and no part of its net earnings benefits any private shareholder or individual,
- The appraiser does not receive any compensation from the association or any other persons for making the appraisal, and
- The fee arrangement is not based in whole or in part on the amount of the appraised value that is allowed as a deduction after an Internal Revenue Service examination or otherwise.

Information included in qualified appraisal. A qualified appraisal must include the following information.

1. A description of the property in sufficient detail for a person who is not generally familiar with the type of property to determine that the property appraised is the property that was (or will be) contributed;

2. The physical condition of any tangible property;

3. The date (or expected date) of contribution;

4. The terms of any agreement or understanding entered into (or expected to be entered into) by or on behalf of the donor and donee that relates to the use, sale, or other disposition of the donated property, including, for example, the terms of any agreement or understanding that:

   a. Temporarily or permanently restricts a donee's right to use or dispose of the donated property;

   b. Earmarks donated property for a particular use; or

   c. Reserves to, or confers upon, anyone (other than a donee organization or an organization participating with a donee organization in cooperative fundraising) any right to the income from the donated property or to the possession of the property, including the right to vote donated securities, to acquire the property by purchase or otherwise, or to designate the person having the income, possession, or right to acquire the property;

5. The name, address, and taxpayer identification number of the qualified appraiser

and, if the appraiser is a partner, an employee, or an independent contractor engaged by a person other than the donor, the name, address, and taxpayer identification number of the partnership or the person who employs or engages the appraiser,

6. The qualifications of the qualified appraiser who signs the appraisal, including the appraiser's background, experience, education, and any membership in professional appraisal associations;

7. A statement that the appraisal was prepared for income tax purposes;

8. The date (or dates) on which the property was valued;

9. The appraised FMV on the date (or expected date) of contribution;

10. The method of valuation used to determine FMV, such as the income approach, the comparable sales or market data approach, or the replacement cost less depreciation approach; and

11. The specific basis for the valuation, such as any specific comparable sales transaction.

Art objects. The following are examples of information that should be included in a description of donated property. These examples are for art objects. A similar detailed breakdown should be given for other property. Appraisals of art objects—paintings in particular—should include all of the following.

1. A complete description of the object, indicating the:

   a. Size,

   b. Subject matter,

   c. Medium,

   d. Name of the artist (or culture), and

   e. Approximate date created.

2. The cost, date, and manner of acquisition.

3. A history of the item, including proof of authenticity.

4. A professional quality image of the object.

5. The facts on which the appraisal was based, such as:

   a. Sales or analyses of similar works by the artist, particularly on or around the valuation date.

   b. Quoted prices in dealer's catalogs of the artist's works or works of other artists of comparable stature.

   c. A record of any exhibitions at which the specific art object had been displayed.

   d. The economic state of the art market at the time of valuation, particularly with respect to the specific property.

   e. The standing of the artist in his profession and in the particular school or time period.

Number of qualified appraisals. A separate qualified appraisal is required for each item

of property that is not included in a group of similar items of property. You need only one qualified appraisal for a group of similar items of property contributed in the same tax year, but you may get separate appraisals for each item. A qualified appraisal for a group of similar items must provide all of the required information for each item of similar property. The appraiser, however, may provide a group description for selected items the total value of which is not more than $100.

Qualified appraiser. A qualified appraiser is an individual with verifiable education and experience in valuing the type of property for which the appraisal is performed.

1. The individual:

   a. Has earned an appraisal designation from a generally recognized professional appraiser organization, or

   b. Has met certain minimum education requirements and two or more years of experience. To meet the minimum education requirement you must have successfully completed professional or college-level coursework obtained from:

      i. A professional or college-level educational organization,

      ii. A professional trade or appraiser organization that regularly offers educational programs in valuing the type of property, or

      iii. An employer as part of an employee apprenticeship or education program similar to professional or college-level courses.

2. The individual regularly prepares appraisals for which he or she is paid.

3. The individual is not an excluded individual.

In addition, the appraiser must make a declaration in the appraisal that, because of his or her background, experience, education, and membership in professional associations, he or she is qualified to make appraisals of the type of property being valued. The appraiser must complete the Declaration of Appraiser section on Form 8283, Section B. More than one appraiser may appraise the property, provided that each complies with the requirements, including signing the qualified appraisal and the Declaration of Appraiser section on Form 8283, Section B.

Excluded individuals. The following individuals cannot be qualified appraisers for the donated property.

1. The donor of the property or the taxpayer who claims the deduction.

2. The donee of the property.

3. A party to the transaction in which the donor acquired the property being appraised, unless the property is donated within 2 months of the date of acquisition and its appraised value is not more than its acquisition price. This applies to the person who sold, exchanged, or gave the property to the donor, or any person who

Publication 561 (February 2020)

Figure 37.3. *(continued)*

acted as an agent for the transferor or donor in the transaction.

4. Any person employed by any of the above persons. For example, if the donor acquired a painting from an art dealer, neither the dealer nor persons employed by the dealer can be qualified appraisers for that painting.

5. Any person related under section 267(b) of the Internal Revenue Code to any of the above persons or married to a person related under section 267(b) to any of the above persons.

6. An appraiser who appraises regularly for a person in (1), (2), or (3), and who does not perform a majority of his or her appraisals made during his or her tax year for other persons.

7. An individual who receives a prohibited appraisal fee for the appraisal of the donated property. See *Prohibited appraisal fee*, earlier.

8. An individual who is prohibited from practicing before the IRS under section 330(c) of title 31 of the United States Code at any time during the 3-year period ending on the date the appraisal is signed by the individual.

In addition, an individual is not a qualified appraiser for a particular donation if the donor had knowledge of facts that would cause a reasonable person to expect the appraiser to falsely overstate the value of the donated property. For example, if the donor and the appraiser make an agreement concerning the amount at which the property will be valued, and the donor knows that amount is more than the FMV of the property, the appraiser is not a qualified appraiser for the donation.

Appraiser penalties. An appraiser who prepares an incorrect appraisal may have to pay a penalty if:

1. The appraiser knows or should have known the appraisal would be used in connection with a return or claim for refund, and

2. The appraisal results in the 20% or 40% penalty for a valuation misstatement described later under *Penalty*.

The penalty imposed on the appraiser is the smaller of:

1. The greater of:

   a. 10% of the underpayment due to the misstatement, or

   b. $1,000, or

2. 125% of the gross income received for the appraisal.

In addition, any appraiser who falsely or fraudulently overstates the value of property described in a qualified appraisal of a Form 8283 that the appraiser has signed may be subject to a civil penalty for aiding and abetting as understatement of tax liability, and may have his or her appraisal disregarded.

Form 8283

Generally, if the claimed deduction for an item of donated property is more than $5,000, you must attach Form 8283 to your tax return and complete Section B.

If you do not attach Form 8283 to your return and complete Section B, the deduction will not be allowed unless your failure was due to reasonable cause, and not willful neglect, or was due to a good faith omission.

You must attach a separate Form 8283 for each item of contributed property that is not part of a group of similar items. If you contribute similar items of property to the same donee organization, you need attach only one Form 8283 for those items. If you contribute similar items of property to more than one donee organization, you must attach a separate form for each donee.

Internal Revenue Service Review of Appraisals

In reviewing an income tax return, the Service may accept the claimed value of the donated property, based on information or appraisals sent with the return, or may make its own determination of FMV. In either case, the Service may:

- Contact the taxpayer to get more information,
- Refer the valuation problem to a Service appraiser or valuation specialist,
- Refer the issue to the Commissioner's Art Advisory Panel (a group of dealers and museum directors who review and recommend acceptance or adjustment of taxpayers' claimed values for major paintings, sculptures, decorative arts, and antiques), or
- Contract with an independent dealer, scholar, or appraiser to appraise the property when the objects require appraisers of highly specialized experience and knowledge.

Responsibility of the Service. The Service is responsible for reviewing appraisals, but it is not responsible for making them. Supporting the FMV listed on your return is your responsibility.

The Service does not accept appraisals without question. Nor does the Service recognize any particular appraiser or organization of appraisers.

Timing of Service action. The Service generally does not approve valuations or appraisals before the actual filing of the tax return to which the appraisal applies. In addition, the Service generally does not issue advance rulings approving or disapproving such appraisals.

Exception. For a request submitted as described earlier under *Art valued at $50,000 or more*, the Service will issue a Statement of Value that can be relied on by the donor of the item of art.

Penalty

You may be liable for a penalty if you overstate the value or adjusted basis of donated property.

20% penalty. The penalty is 20% of the underpayment of tax related to the overstatement if:

- The value or adjusted basis claimed on the return is 150% or more of the correct amount, and
- You underpaid your tax by more than $5,000 because of the overstatement.

40% penalty. The penalty is 40%, rather than 20%, if:

- The value or adjusted basis claimed on the return is 200% or more of the correct amount, and
- You underpaid your tax by more than $5,000 because of the overstatement.

How To Get Tax Help

If you have questions about a tax issue, need help preparing your tax return, or want to download free publications, forms, or instructions, go to IRS.gov and find resources that can help you right away.

Preparing and filing your tax return. After receiving your wage and earning statements (Form W-2, W-2G, 1099-R, 1099-MISC) from all employers and interest and dividend statements from banks (Forms 1099), you can find free options to prepare and file your return on IRS.gov or in your local community if you qualify.

The Volunteer Income Tax Assistance (VITA) program offers free tax help to people with low-to-moderate incomes, persons with disabilities, and limited-English-speaking taxpayers who need help preparing their own tax returns. The Tax Counseling for the Elderly (TCE) program offers free tax help for all taxpayers, particularly those who are 60 years of age and older. TCE volunteers specialize in answering questions about pensions and retirement-related issues unique to seniors.

You can go to IRS.gov to see your options for preparing and filing your return, which include the following.

- **Free File.** Go to *IRS.gov/FreeFile* to see if you qualify to use brand-name software to prepare and *e-file* your federal tax return for free.
- **VITA.** Go to *IRS.gov/VITA*, download the free IRS2Go app, or call 800-906-9887 to find the nearest VITA location for free tax return preparation.
- **TCE.** Go to *IRS.gov/TCE*, download the free IRS2Go app, or call 888-227-7669 to find the nearest TCE location for free tax return preparation.

Employers can register to use Business Services Online. The SSA offers online service for fast, free, and secure online W-2 filing options to CPAs, accountants, enrolled agents, and individuals who process Forms W-2, Wage

Figure 37.3. *(continued)*

and Tax Statement, and Forms W-2c, Corrected Wage and Tax Statement. Employers can go to *SSA.gov/employer* for more information.

 Getting answers to your tax questions. On IRS.gov, get answers to your tax questions anytime, anywhere.

- Go to *IRS.gov/Help* for a variety of tools that will help you get answers to some of the most common tax questions.
- Go to *IRS.gov/ITA* for the Interactive Tax Assistant, a tool that will ask you questions on a number of tax law topics and provide answers. You can print the entire interview and the final response for your records.
- Go to *IRS.gov/Forms* to search for our forms, instructions, and publications. You will find details on 2019 tax changes and hundreds of interactive links to help you find answers to your questions.
- You may also be able to access tax law information in your electronic filing software.

Tax reform. Tax reform legislation affects individuals, businesses, and tax-exempt and government entities. Go to *IRS.gov/TaxReform* for information and updates on how this legislation affects your taxes.

IRS social media. Go to *IRS.gov/SocialMedia* to see the various social media tools the IRS uses to share the latest information on tax changes, scam alerts, initiatives, products, and services. At the IRS, privacy and security are paramount. We use these tools to share public information with you. **Don't** post your social security number or other confidential information on social media sites. Always protect your identity when using any social networking site.

The following IRS YouTube channels provide short, informative videos on various tax-related topics in English, Spanish, and ASL.
- *Youtube.com/irsvideos*.
- *Youtube.com/irsvideosmultilingua*.
- *Youtube.com/irsvideosASL*.

Watching IRS videos. The IRS Video portal (*IRSVideos.gov*) contains video and audio presentations for individuals, small businesses, and tax professionals.

Getting tax information in other languages. For taxpayers whose native language isn't English, we have the following resources available. Taxpayers can find information on IRS.gov in the following languages.
- *Spanish* (*IRS.gov/Spanish*).
- *Chinese* (*IRS.gov/Chinese*).
- *Korean* (*IRS.gov/Korean*).
- *Russian* (*IRS.gov/Russian*).
- *Vietnamese* (*IRS.gov/Vietnamese*).

The IRS Taxpayer Assistance Centers (TACs) provide over-the-phone interpreter service in over 170 languages, and the service is available free to taxpayers.

Getting tax forms and publications. Go to *IRS.gov/Forms* to view, download, or print all of the forms, instructions, and publications you may need. You can also download and view popular tax publications and instructions (including the 1040 and 1040-SR instructions) on mobile devices as an eBook at no charge at *IRS.gov/eBooks*. Or you can go to *IRS.gov/OrderForms* to place an order and have them mailed to you within 10 business days.

Access your online account (individual taxpayers only). Go to *IRS.gov/Account* to securely access information about your federal tax account.
- View the amount you owe, pay online, or set up an online payment agreement.
- Access your tax records online.
- Review the past 24 months of your payment history.
- Go to *IRS.gov/SecureAccess* to review the required identity authentication process.

Using direct deposit. The fastest way to receive a tax refund is to combine direct deposit and IRS *e-file*. Direct deposit securely and electronically transfers your refund directly into your financial account. Eight in 10 taxpayers use direct deposit to receive their refund. The IRS issues more than 90% of refunds in less than 21 days.

Getting a transcript or copy of a return. The quickest way to get a copy of your tax transcript is to go to *IRS.gov/Transcripts*. Click on either "Get Transcript Online" or "Get Transcript by Mail" to order a copy of your transcript. If you prefer, you can order your transcript by calling 800-908-9946.

Using online tools to help prepare your return. Go to *IRS.gov/Tools* for the following.
- The *Earned Income Tax Credit Assistant* (*IRS.gov/EITCAssistant*) determines if you're eligible for the EIC.
- The *Online EIN Application* (*IRS.gov/EIN*) helps you get an employer identification number.
- The *Tax Withholding Estimator* (*IRS.gov/W4app*) makes it easier for everyone to pay the correct amount of tax during the year. The Estimator replaces the Withholding Calculator. The redesigned tool is a convenient, online way to check and tailor your withholding. It's more user-friendly for taxpayers, including retirees and self-employed individuals. The new and improved features include the following.
  - Easy to understand language;
  - The ability to switch between screens, correct previous entries, and skip screens that don't apply;
  - Tips and links to help you determine if you qualify for tax credits and deductions;
  - A progress tracker;
  - A self-employment tax feature; and
  - Automatic calculation of taxable social security benefits.
- The *First Time Homebuyer Credit Account Look-up* (*IRS.gov/HomeBuyer*) tool provides information on your repayments and account balance.
- The *Sales Tax Deduction Calculator* (*IRS.gov/SalesTax*) figures the amount you can claim if you itemize deductions on Schedule A (Form 1040 or 1040-SR), choose not to claim state and local income taxes, and you didn't save your receipts showing the sales tax you paid.

Resolving tax-related identity theft issues.
- The IRS doesn't initiate contact with taxpayers by email or telephone to request personal or financial information. This includes any type of electronic communication, such as text messages and social media channels.
- Go to *IRS.gov/IDProtection* for information.
- If your SSN has been lost or stolen or you suspect you're a victim of tax-related identity theft, visit *IRS.gov/IdentityTheft* to learn what steps you should take.

Checking on the status of your refund.
- Go to *IRS.gov/Refunds*.
- The IRS can't issue refunds before mid-February 2020 for returns that claimed the EIC or the ACTC. This applies to the entire refund, not just the portion associated with these credits.
- Download the official IRS2Go app to your mobile device to check your refund status.
- Call the automated refund hotline at 800-829-1954.

Making a tax payment. The IRS uses the latest encryption technology to ensure your electronic payments are safe and secure. You can make electronic payments online, by phone, and from a mobile device using the IRS2Go app. Paying electronically is quick, easy, and faster than mailing in a check or money order. Go to *IRS.gov/Payments* to make a payment using any of the following options.
- *IRS Direct Pay*: Pay your individual tax bill or estimated tax payment directly from your checking or savings account at no cost to you.
- *Debit or Credit Card*: Choose an approved payment processor to pay online, by phone, and by mobile device.
- *Electronic Funds Withdrawal*: Offered only when filing your federal taxes using tax return preparation software or through a tax professional.
- *Electronic Federal Tax Payment System*: Best option for businesses. Enrollment is required.
- *Check or Money Order*: Mail your payment to the address listed on the notice or instructions.
- *Cash*: You may be able to pay your taxes with cash at a participating retail store.
- *Same-Day Wire*: You may be able to do same-day wire from your financial institution. Contact your financial institution for availability, cost, and cut-off times.

What if I can't pay now? Go to *IRS.gov/Payments* for more information about your options.
- Apply for an *online payment agreement* (*IRS.gov/OPA*) to meet your tax obligation in monthly installments if you can't pay your taxes in full today. Once you complete the online process, you will receive immediate notification of whether your agreement has been approved.
- Use the *Offer in Compromise Pre-Qualifier* to see if you can settle your tax debt for less than the full amount you owe. For more information on the Offer in Compromise program, go to *IRS.gov/OIC*.

Page 12

Publication 561 (February 2020)

Figure 37.3. (*continued*)

Checking the status of an amended return. Go to *IRS.gov/WMAR* to track the status of Form 1040-X amended returns. Please note that it can take up to 3 weeks from the date you mailed your amended return for it to show up in our system, and processing it can take up to 16 weeks.

Understanding an IRS notice or letter. Go to *IRS.gov/Notices* to find additional information about responding to an IRS notice or letter.

Contacting your local IRS office. Keep in mind, many questions can be answered on IRS.gov without visiting an IRS Taxpayer Assistance Center (TAC). Go to *IRS.gov/LetUsHelp* for the topics people ask about most. If you still need help, IRS TACs provide tax help when a tax issue can't be handled online or by phone. All TACs now provide service by appointment so you'll know in advance that you can get the service you need without long wait times. Before you visit, go to *IRS.gov/TACLocator* to find the nearest TAC, check hours, available services, and appointment options. Or, on the IRS2Go app, under the Stay Connected tab, choose the Contact Us option and click on "Local Offices."

The Taxpayer Advocate Service (TAS) Is Here To Help You
What Is TAS?

TAS is an *independent* organization within the IRS that helps taxpayers and protects taxpayer rights. Their job is to ensure that every taxpayer is treated fairly and that you know and understand your rights under the *Taxpayer Bill of Rights*.

How Can You Learn About Your Taxpayer Rights?

The Taxpayer Bill of Rights describes 10 basic rights that all taxpayers have when dealing with the IRS. Go to *TaxpayerAdvocate.IRS.gov* to help you understand *what these rights mean to you* and how they apply. These are *your* rights. Know them. Use them.

What Can TAS Do For You?

TAS can help you resolve problems that you can't resolve with the IRS. And their service is free. If you qualify for their assistance, you will be assigned to one advocate who will work with you throughout the process and will do everything possible to resolve your issue. TAS can help you if:

- Your problem is causing financial difficulty for you, your family, or your business;
- You face (or your business is facing) an immediate threat of adverse action; or
- You've tried repeatedly to contact the IRS but no one has responded, or the IRS hasn't responded by the date promised.

How Can You Reach TAS?

TAS has offices *in every state, the District of Columbia, and Puerto Rico*. Your local advocate's number is in your local directory and at *TaxpayerAdvocate.IRS.gov/Contact-Us*. You can also call them at 877-777-4778.

How Else Does TAS Help Taxpayers?

TAS works to resolve large-scale problems that affect many taxpayers. If you know of one of these broad issues, please report it to them at *IRS.gov/SAMS*.

TAS also has a website, *Tax Reform Changes*, which shows you how the new tax law may change your future tax filings and helps you plan for these changes. The information is categorized by tax topic in the order of the IRS Form 1040 or 1040-SR. Go to *TaxChanges.us* for more information.

TAS for Tax Professionals

TAS can provide a variety of information for tax professionals, including tax law updates and guidance, TAS programs, and ways to let TAS know about systemic problems you've seen in your practice.

Low Income Taxpayer Clinics (LITCs)

LITCs are independent from the IRS. LITCs represent individuals whose income is below a certain level and need to resolve tax problems with the IRS, such as audits, appeals, and tax collection disputes. In addition, clinics can provide information about taxpayer rights and responsibilities in different languages for individuals who speak English as a second language. Services are offered for free or a small fee. To find a clinic near you, visit *IRS.gov/LITC* or see IRS Pub. 4134, *Low Income Taxpayer Clinic List*.

Figure 37.3.   *(continued)*

To help us develop a more useful index, please let us know if you have ideas for index entries.
See "Comments and Suggestions" in the "Introduction" for the ways you can reach us.

Publication 561 (February 2020)

Figure 37.3. (continued)

IRS Updated Publication Citations for Charitable Contributions

Treas. Reg. § 1.170A–17 § 1.170A–17. **Qualified appraisal and qualified appraiser** (www.appraisers.org/docs/default-source/discipline_pp/1170a17-qualified-appraisal-and-qualified-appraiser.pdf?sfvrsn=2)

- Notice 2006-96 (www.irs.gov/pub/irs-drop/n-06-96.pdf)

- 26 IRS Code § 170; Reg. 1.170A (www.irs.gov/pub/irs-drop/rr-03-28.pdf)

Final Regulations for Non-cash Charitable Contributions (www.federalregister.gov/documents/2018/07/30/2018-15734/substantiation-and-reporting-requirements-for-cash-and-noncash-charitable-contribution-deductions)

- Rev. Proc. 96-15 (www.irs.gov/pub/irs-drop/rp96-15.pdf)

- Publication 561 (www.irs.gov/pub/irs-pdf/p561.pdf) (Rev. February 2020)

- Publication 526 (www.irs.gov/pub/irs-pdf/p526.pdf) (Rev. April 2020)

- IRS Form 8283 (www.irs.gov/pub/irs-pdf/f8283.pdf) (Rev. November 2019)

- IRS Form 8283 instructions (www.irs.gov/pub/irs-pdf/i8283.pdf)

- Every appraisal performed in connection with a noncash charitable contribution must include the following disclosure: "I understand that my appraisal will be used in connection with a return or claim for refund. I also understand that, if there is a substantial or gross valuation misstatement of the value of the property claimed on the return or claim for refund that is based on my appraisal, I may be subject to a penalty under section 6695A of the Internal Revenue Code, as well as other applicable penalties. I affirm that I have not been at any time in the three-year period ending on the date of the appraisal barred from presenting evidence or testimony before the Department of the Treasury or the Internal Revenue Service pursuant to 31 U.S.C. 330(c)."

- Where the appraisal is performed after the contribution is made to the museum, the valuation effective date cannot be later than the date on which the contribution was made and cannot be more than sixty days before the contribution is to be made.

CHAPTER 38

FAQs Regarding Gifts of Property

ROMY M. VREELAND

THE FOLLOWING ARE SOME COMMONLY ASKED questions concerning gifts of property, asked by donors and donees alike. Please use these answers as guidance, but realize that they should not take the place of advice given to you by your legal, financial, or tax adviser, who has your particular interests, as well as current laws, in mind.

Who signs Form 8283 on behalf of the donee?

According to the instructions for Form 8283, "The person acknowledging a gift must be an official authorized to sign the tax returns of the organization, or a person specifically designated to sign Form 8283." Donee institutions should refer to their governing documents to determine who is authorized to sign Form 8283.

What information needs to be filled in on Form 8283 before the donee signs? Does the donor and/or appraiser need to sign Form 8283 before the donee?

According to the instructions for Form 8283, the donor must complete at least his or her "name, identifying number, and description of the donated property (line 5, column (a)" in part I of section B before sending the form to the donee for signature. The condition of the property at the time of its donation must also be indicated for tangible property. Part II, the taxpayer statement, must also be completed, if required, before the form is sent to the donee. The appraiser can sign before or after the donee.

Can the donee require, or must the donee see, an appraisal attached to Form 8283 it has been asked to sign?

The donee need not see the appraisal, or even a stated value on Form 8283, before signing part IV of the form, since the donee needs only to confirm that it received the described property from the named donor and whether or not it will be put to an unrelated use, and the date on which it received the property. Some institutions require a copy of an appraisal from the donor for the institution's records, but this is not required by the IRS. The donor and/or the museum often request a copy for the museum files, and most appraisers can provide a complete copy of the appraisal, in print or electronic format.

How does the donee determine what to enter as the "received" date?

The "received" date must be entered by the donee in section IV of Form 8283. This date is the date that the donee received title to the donated property, which may be the same date or later than the date on which it took physical possession of the property. The donee should look to its governing policies (such as its by-laws or collections management policy) to determine when a gift is formally accepted, since the procedure varies among institutions.

Do artist donations require a Form 8283? I heard artists can only deduct the cost of materials used in creating an artwork.

An artist's tax deduction on a donation of his or her own work is limited to the artist's cost basis, as the work is considered ordinary income property. An artist must file Form 8283 for the donation if the amount of the deduction exceeds $500. If the deduction is greater than $5,000, the donee must fill in and sign part IV, just as it would for other donations valued by the donor above $5,000.

Can the date of receipt of a gift be changed by a donee at the donor's request?

A date of receipt of a gift should be specific and should not be changed by a donee institution after a gift is accepted, except in the case of a documented error. Should the date of a donation be called into question by the IRS, the donee's records must be clear. Consistency in recording the date of acceptance is key to a donee's gift acceptance policy.

When does the appraisal need to be dated/completed in order to be accepted by the IRS?

According to IRS rules, an appraisal cannot be dated more than sixty days before the receipt of the donation by the donee and cannot be dated after the due date of the donor's tax return.

A donor has not returned a signed deed/offer letter/receipt letter, and I, as donee, am unsure whether to consider the gift valid. What can I do?

Review the documentation you do have on the gift. If your documentation shows the property owner's donative intent, even if it is not on your usual form, this should be enough to proceed with processing the gift as usual. When in doubt, contact your institution's lawyer for an opinion on whether donative intent is clear and the gift can be completed. If a person has left property at your institution and becomes unreachable before completing gift paperwork, check your state's laws regarding abandoned property. You may be able to claim title to the property in lieu of a gift.

As a donor, I have asked the donee to supply me with their value of my donated property so I can use it for tax purposes. Why won't they supply it?

Under IRS rules, a donee is considered an "excluded individual" and cannot be considered a qualified appraiser. See IRS Publication 561: Determining the Value of Donated Property.

As a donee, I do not agree with the valuation a donor has indicated for the donated property on a Form 8283 that I have been asked to sign. What should I do?

Form 8283 expressly states that the donee's signature in section IV does not indicate agreement with the donor's valuation of the donated property. The donee should also be wary of giving what could be construed as tax advice to a donor. However, if the institution wishes to approach the donor either out of concern that the appraisal will not hold up to IRS scrutiny or to prevent a potential controversy (or both), it should consult with its own tax adviser on how to proceed.

As a donee, do I need to supply a deed of gift to a vendor who wishes to make a bargain sale to the museum?

No. In a bargain sale transaction, the gift is inherent in the sale of the property, so no deed is required, nor would it be appropriate. The donee will need to supply the vendor with a receipt or an acknowledgment letter for the gift, however, which can be substantially similar to those used for other gifts of property.

As a donor/vendor, I wish to make a bargain sale to an institution. How does the paperwork differ from an ordinary sale?

The invoice sent to the institution should be similar to an invoice for an ordinary sale, except that the words "bargain sale" should appear. After payment is made, you can expect to receive a gift receipt from the donee, and you may have to fill out an IRS Form 8283 if you wish to claim a tax deduction for the gift portion of the bargain sale.

CHAPTER 39
IRS Revenue Procedure 96-15

COMPILED AND EDITED BY LAURETTE E. MCCARTHY

IRS Revenue Procedure 96-15 Part III

Administrative, Procedural and Miscellaneous

26 CFR 601.201: Rulings and determination letters. (Also part I, §§ 170, 2031, 2512; l.170A-13; 20.2031-6; 25.2512-1.)

SECTION 1. PURPOSE

This revenue procedure informs taxpayers how to request from the Internal Revenue Service a Statement of Value that can be used to substantiate the value of art for income, estate, or gift tax purposes. A taxpayer that complies with the provisions of this revenue procedure may rely on the Statement of Value in completing the taxpayer's federal income tax, estate tax, or gift tax return that reports the transfer of art.

SECTION 2. BACKGROUND

.01 Income Tax Charitable Deduction.

(1) Section 170(a) of the Internal Revenue Code allows as a deduction any charitable contribution (as defined in § 170(c)) payment of which is made during the taxable year.

(2) Section 1.170A-l(c)(l) of the Income Tax Regulations provides that if a charitable contribution is made in property other than money, the amount of the contribution is generally the fair market value of the property at the time of the contribution.

(3) Section 1.170A-l(c)(2) provides that the fair market value is the price at which the property would change hands between a willing buyer and a willing seller, neither being under any compulsion to buy or sell and both having reasonable knowledge of the relevant facts.

(4) Section 1.170A-13 sets forth the recordkeeping and return requirements for deductions for charitable contributions. For a deduction for a charitable contribution of property in excess of $5,000, § 1.170A-13(c) requires a qualified appraisal and an appraisal summary.

(5) Rev. Proc. 66-49, 1966-2 C.B. 1257, provides guidelines for review of appraisals of contributed property for purposes of § 170. Section 4.01 of Rev. Proc. 66-49 states that the Service will not approve valuations or appraisals prior to the actual filing of the tax return to which the appraisal pertains, and will not issue advance rulings approving or disapproving appraisals.

.02 Estate Tax.

(1) Section 2031 provides that the value of the gross estate of a decedent is determined by including the value at the time of death of all property wherever situated.

(2) Section 20.2031-l(b) of the Estate Tax Regulations provides that the value of property includible in a decedent's gross estate is its fair market value at the time of the decedent's death.

(3) Section 2032(a) provides that the executor may elect to determine the value of all the property included in the gross estate as of six months after the decedent's death. However, property distributed, sold, exchanged, or otherwise disposed of within six months after death must be valued as of the date of distribution, sale, exchange, or other disposition.

(4) Section 20.2031-6(a) provides that the fair market value of a decedent's household and personal effects is the price that a willing buyer would pay to a willing seller, neither being under any compulsion to buy or to sell and both having reasonable knowledge of the relevant facts.

(5) Section 20.2031-6(b) provides that if there are included among the household and personal effects articles having marked artistic or intrinsic value of a total in excess of $3,000, the appraisal of an expert or experts, under oath, must be filed with the estate tax return.

(6) Section 20.2031-6(d) provides that if, pursuant to § 20.2031-6 (a) and (b), expert appraisers are employed, care must be taken to see that they are reputable and of recognized competency to appraise the particular class of property involved. In listing paintings having artistic value, the size, subject, and artist's name must be stated.

03 Gift Tax.

(1) Section 2512(a) provides that if a gift is made in property, the value thereof at the date of the gift is the amount of the gift.

(2) Section 25.2512-1 of the Gift Tax Regulations provides that the value of property is the price at which the property would change hands between a willing buyer and a willing seller, neither being under any compulsion to buy or to sell and both having reasonable knowledge of the relevant facts.

.04 Legislation Authorizing User Fees. Section 10511 of the Revenue Act of 1987, 1987-3 C.B. 1, 166, as amended by § 11319 of the Omnibus Budget Reconciliation Act of 1990, 1991-2 C.B. 481,511, and by § 743 of the Uruguay Round Agreements Act, 1995-111.R.B. 5, 14, requires the Secretary of the Treasury or delegate to establish a program requiring the payment of user fees for requests to the Service for letter rulings, opinion letters, determination letters, and similar requests. The fees apply to requests made on or after February 1, 1988, and before October 1, 2000. The fees charged under the program (1) vary according to categories or subcategories established by the secretary; (2) are determined after taking into account the average time for, and difficulty of, complying with requests in each category and subcategory; and (3) are payable in advance.

SECTION 3. SCOPE

.01 Except as provided in section 3.02, this revenue procedure applies to an item of art that has been appraised at $50,000 or more, and has been transferred (1) as a "charitable contribution" within the meaning of § 170(c), (2) by reason of a decedent's death, or (3) by inter vivos gift.

.02 The Service may issue a Statement of Value for items appraised at less than $50,000 if (1) the request for the Statement of Value includes a request for appraisal review for at least one item appraised at $50,000 or more, and (2) the Service determines that issuance of such a Statement would be in the best interest of efficient tax administration.

.03 The Service may decline to issue a Statement of Value when appropriate in the interest of efficient tax administration. If the Service declines to issue a Statement of Value under this section 3.03, the Service will refund the user fee.

SECTION 4. DEFINITIONS

.01 The term "art" includes paintings, sculpture, watercolors, prints, drawings, ceramics, antique furniture, decorative arts, textiles, carpets, silver, rare manuscripts, historical memorabilia, and other similar objects.

.02 The term "taxpayer" includes an executor or administrator acting on behalf of an estate, and a donor of a gift.

.03 The term "valuation date" refers to the date of death, the alternate valuation date (as established under§ 2032(a)), or the date of the gift.

SECTION 5. REQUESTING A STATEMENT OF VALUE FOR INCOME TAX CHARITABLE DEDUCTION PURPOSES

.01 To request a Statement of Value from the Service for an item of art transferred as a charitable contribution within the meaning of § 170(c), a taxpayer must submit to the Service a request for a Statement of Value for the item prior to filing the income tax return that first reports the charitable contribution. The request must include the following:

(1) a copy of an appraisal (as described in his revenue procedure) of the item of art;

(2) a check or money order payable to the Internal Revenue Service (user fee) in the amount of $6,500 for a request for a Statement of Value for one, two, or three items of art, plus $350 for each additional item of art for which a Statement of Value is requested;

(3) a completed appraisal summary (section B of Form 8283, Noncash Charitable Contributions) that meets the requirements of § l.170A-13(c)(4); and

(4) the location of the district office that has or will have examination jurisdiction over the return (not the service center where the return is filed).

.02 A taxpayer may withdraw the request for a Statement of Value at any time before it is issued by the Service. The user fee will not be refunded for a request that is withdrawn. When a request is withdrawn, the appropriate district director will be notified.

.03 If a request for a Statement of Value lacks information essential to the issuance of a Statement of Value for an item of art, the Service will notify the taxpayer that the request will not be processed for that item unless the Service receives the missing information within thirty calendar days after the date of such notification.

SECTION 6. APPRAISAL FOR INCOME TAX CHARITABLE DEDUCTION PURPOSES

.01 An appraisal submitted to the Service by a taxpayer under section 5 of this revenue procedure must meet the requirements for a qualified appraisal under § 1.170A-13(c)(3)(i)- (iii), and must also include the following:

(1) a complete description of the item of art, including:

(a) the name of the artist or culture,

(b) the title or subject matter,

(c) the medium, such as oil on canvas, or watercolor on paper,

(d) the date created,

(e) the size,

(f) any marks, signatures, or labels on the item of art, on the back of the item of art, or affixed to the frame,

(g) the history (provenance) of the item, including proof of authenticity, if that information is available,

(h) a record of any exhibitions at which the item was displayed,

(i) any reference source citing the item, and

(j) the physical condition of the item;

(2) a professional quality photograph of a size and quality fully showing the item, preferably an 8 x 10 inch color photograph or a color transparency not smaller than 4 x 5 inches; and

(3) the specific basis for the valuation.

.02 The appraisal must be made no earlier than sixty days prior to the date of the contribution of the item of art.

.03 Taxpayers are encouraged to include in the request any additional information that may affect the determination of the fair market value of the item of art.

.04 The requirements of section 6 of this revenue procedure must be met by subchapter C corporations, even though they would otherwise be exempt under$ 1.170A-13(c)(2)(ii)(B)(3) from the appraisal requirements.

SECTION 7. REQUESTING A STATEMENT OF VALUE FOR ESTATE TAX OR GIFT TAX PURPOSES

.01 To request a Statement of Value from the Service for an item of art transferred as part of an estate or as an inter vivos gift, a taxpayer must submit to the Service a request for a Statement of Value for the item prior to filing the federal estate tax return or the federal gift tax return that first reports the transfer of the item. The request must include the following:

(1) a copy of an appraisal (as described in section 8 of this revenue procedure) of the item of art;

(2) a check or money order payable to the Internal Revenue Service (user fee) in the amount of $7,500 for a request for a Statement of Value for one, two, or three items of art, plus $400 for each additional item of art for which a Statement of Value is requested;

(3) a description of the item of art;

(4) the appraised fair market value;

(5) the cost, date, and manner of acquisition;

(6) the date of death (or the alternate valuation date, if applicable) or the date of the gift; and

(7) the location of the district office that has or will have examination jurisdiction over the return (not the service center where the return is filed).

.02 A taxpayer may withdraw the request for a Statement of Value at any time before it is issued by the Service. The user fee will not be refunded for a request that is withdrawn. When a request is withdrawn, the appropriate district director will be notified.

.03 If a request for a Statement of Value lacks information essential to the issuance of a Statement of Value for an item of art, the Service will notify the taxpayer that the request will not be processed for that item unless the Service receives the missing information within thirty calendar days after the date of such notification.

SECTION 8. APPRAISAL FOR ESTATE TAX OR GIFT TAX PURPOSES

.01 An appraisal submitted to the Service by a taxpayer under section 7 of this revenue procedure must include the following:

(1) a complete description of the item of art, including:

(a) the name of the artist or culture,

(b) the title or subject matter,

(c) the medium, such as oil on canvas, or watercolor on paper,

(d) the date created,

(e) the size,

(f) any marks, signatures, or labels on the item of art, on the back of the item of art, or affixed to the frame,

(g) the history (provenance) of the item, including proof of authenticity, if such information is available,

(h) a record of any exhibitions at which the item was displayed,

(i) any reference source citing the item, and

(j) the physical condition of the item;

(2) a professional quality photograph of a size and quality fully showing the item, preferably an 8 × 10 inch color photograph or a color transparency not smaller than 4 × 5 inches;

(3) a statement that the appraisal was prepared for estate tax purposes or gift tax purposes;

(4) the date (or dates) on which the item of art was appraised;

(5) the appraised fair market value (within the meaning of § 20.2031-6(a) or 25.2512-1); and

(6) the specific basis for the valuation.

.02 The appraisal must be made no earlier than sixty days prior to the valuation date.

.03 Taxpayers are encouraged to include in the request any additional information that may affect the determination of the fair market value of the item of art.

.04 An appraisal must:

(1) be prepared, signed, and dated by an appraiser, and contain a statement by the appraiser that:

(a) the appraiser either holds himself or herself out to the public as an appraiser or performs appraisals on a regular basis;

(b) the appraiser is qualified to make appraisals of the item of art;

(c) the appraiser is not the taxpayer;

(d) the appraiser was not a party to the transaction in which the decedent or donor of the gift acquired the item of art being appraised, unless the valuation date is within two months of the date of acquisition and the appraised value is not less than the acquisition price;

(e) the appraiser is not the beneficiary or donee receiving the item of art;

(f) the appraiser is not a person who was employed by the decedent or is employed by the taxpayer;

(g) the appraiser is not related to any of the foregoing persons under § 267(6) or married to a person who is in a relationship described in § 267(6) with any of the foregoing persons;

(h) the appraiser is not an appraiser who was regularly used by the decedent or who is regularly used by the taxpayer or the beneficiary or donee; and

(i) the appraisal fee is not based on the appraised value of the item of art;

(2) include the name, address, and taxpayer identification number (if a taxpayer identification number is otherwise required by § 6109 and the regulations thereunder) of the appraiser. If the appraiser is acting in his or her capacity as a partner in a partnership, an employee of any person (whether an individual, corporation, or partnership), or an independent contractor engaged by a person other than the taxpayer, the appraiser must include the name, address, and

taxpayer identification number (if a taxpayer identification number is otherwise required by § 6109 and the regulations thereunder) of the partnership or the person who employs or engages the appraiser; and

(3) include the qualifications of the appraiser who signs the appraisal, including the appraiser's background, experience, education, and membership, if any, in professional appraisal associations.

.05 The appraisal will not satisfy the requirements of this section if the taxpayer has knowledge of facts that would cause a reasonable person to expect the appraiser to overstate or understate the value of the item of art.

SECTION 9. TAXPAYER'S DECLARATION

.01 A request to obtain a Statement of Value, any factual representations associated with the request, and any amendments to the request must be accompanied by the following declaration: "Under penalties of perjury, I declare that I have examined this request, including the accompanying documents, and to the best of my knowledge and belief, the facts presented in support of this request are true, correct, and complete."

.02 The declaration must be signed by the taxpayer, and not the taxpayer's representative. The person signing for an estate must be the executor or administrator of the estate. The person signing for a trust or partnership must be a trustee or general partner who has personal knowledge of the facts. The person signing for a corporate taxpayer must be an officer of the corporate taxpayer who has personal knowledge of the facts. If a corporate taxpayer is a member of an affiliated group filing consolidated returns, a penalties-of-perjury statement must also be signed and submitted by an officer of the common parent of the group.

.03 A taxpayer that submits additional factual information on several occasions may provide one declaration that refers to all submissions.

SECTION 10. WHERE TO SUBMIT REQUESTS

Send requests for a Statement of Value to the address listed below.

Internal Revenue Service/Art Appraisal Services

1111 Constitution Ave., Suite 700

C:AP:SO:ART

Washington, DC 20224-0002

ATTN: AAS

Note: it is recommended that a private delivery service be utilized, as packages sent via USPS are subject to irradiation that may damage professional photographs.

SECTION 11. NATIONAL OFFICE CONSIDERATION OF REQUESTS

.01 For a completed request for a Statement of Value received after July 15, but on or before January 15, the Service will ordinarily issue a Statement of Value by the following June 30. For a completed request for a Statement of Value received after January 15, but on or before July 15, the Service will ordinarily issue a Statement of Value by the following December 31. It is the responsibility of taxpayers to obtain extensions, as necessary, to file the appropriate tax returns.

.02 If the Service agrees with the value reported on the taxpayer's appraisal, the Service will issue a Statement of Value approving the appraisal.

.03 If the Service disagrees with the value reported on the taxpayer's appraisal, the Service will issue a Statement of Value with the Service's determination of value, and the basis for its disagreement with the taxpayer's appraisal.

SECTION 12. ATTACHMENT OF STATEMENT OF VALUE TO RETURN

.01 A copy of the Statement of Value, regardless of whether the taxpayer agrees with it, must be attached to and filed with the taxpayer's income, estate, or gift tax return that reports the transfer of the item of art valued in the Statement of Value. However, if, prior to receiving a Statement of Value, the taxpayer files an income, estate, or gift tax return reporting the transfer of an item of art for which a Statement of Value was requested, the taxpayer must indicate on the return that a Statement of Value has been requested and attach a copy of the request to the return. Upon receipt of the Statement of Value, the taxpayer must file an amended income or gift tax return, or a supplemental estate tax return, with the Statement of Value attached.

.02 If a taxpayer disagrees with a Statement of Value issued by the Service, the taxpayer may submit with the tax return additional information in support of a different value.

SECTION 13. EFFECT OF STATEMENT OF VALUE

.01 A taxpayer may rely on a Statement of Value received from the Service for an item of art, except as provided in sections 13.02 and 13.03 of this revenue procedure.

.02 A taxpayer may not rely on a Statement of Value issued to another taxpayer.

INTERNAL REVENUE SERVICE
OFFICE OF ART APPRAISAL SERVICES
Washington, DC

Photographic Requirements for Art, Antiques,
Decorative Arts & Other Cultural Properties
Reviewed by Art Appraisal Services and
The Commissioner's Art Advisory Panel

The Office of Art Appraisal Services (AAS) and the Commissioner's Art Advisory Panel determine the fair market value of thousands of fine and decorative art objects and other cultural properties based on photographic images and appraisals provided by the taxpayer. Consequently, professional quality color photographs and/or high resolution digital images of the subject properties are crucial for our review. Cases submitted without photographs **cannot** be processed in a timely manner. We encourage use of a professional photographer.

Please request that the taxpayer (or representative) provide a color image of each property with a claimed value of $50,000 or more in one of the acceptable photographic formats listed below. Each object should be shown in its entirety with separate images depicting important details, such as the artist's signature, date, labels or other distinguishing features (including damage and repairs). Multiple views are helpful for 3-dimensional works of art.

ACCEPTABLE FORMATS:

➢ **PHOTOGRAPHS:** Clear, **professional-quality** 8" x 10" color photographs printed on photographic paper.

➢ **DIGITAL IMAGES:** High resolution color digital images (labeled with descriptive information) may be submitted on a CD together with a printed image of each object. *(Thumbnail size images are acceptable only for identification purposes.)* AAS does not require a minimum pixel count, but rather stresses the need for high resolution images printed professionally on photographic paper to produce sharp photographs.

➢ **NOTE:** All photographs and digital images submitted to AAS should be labeled with the taxpayer's appraisal object number, artist's name, and title.

UNACCEPTABLE FORMATS:

➢ Blurry or dark photographs
➢ Photos where the subject is obscured by glare or flash
➢ Photos cropping out part of the subject or shot too far away
➢ Photos smaller than 8" x 10"
➢ Low resolution digital images
➢ Photos printed on substandard printers
➢ Photos printed on low-grade paper *(i.e. copier paper)*
➢ Photocopies
➢ Transparencies

Figure 39.1. IRS Photographic Requirements for Art, Antiques, Decorative Arts, and Cultural Property. Effective date January 1, 2019.

.03 A taxpayer may not rely on a Statement of Value if the representations upon which the Statement of Value was based are not accurate statements of the material facts.

SECTION 14. EFFECT ON OTHER DOCUMENTS
Rev. Proc. 66-49 is modified.

SECTION 15. EFFECTIVE DATE
This revenue procedure applies to a request for a Statement of Value for an item of art if the request is submitted after January 15, 1996.

REASONING FOR APPRAISED VALUE: The appraisal of each work should provide the basis or reasoning as to how the appraiser arrived at the individual appraised value. Individual comparable sales should be included. These sales should be analyzed in terms of quality, and so on and discussed as to how they relate to the subject property. The item discussion should include commentary regarding any special conditions or circumstances about the property, and a discussion of the quality or importance of the property in relation to other works of art by the same artist, and of the state of the art market at the time of valuation. Whenever possible, statements should be supported with factual evidence.

Note: It is understood that complete information will not be readily available in every case. However, the validity of the appraiser's valuation is enhanced and the IRS's appraisal review facilitated by complete and accurate information. This object identification should be accompanied by a professional-quality photograph of the subject property (see photographic requirements).

New IRS Definition of a Qualified Appraiser

§ 1.170A–17 (b) Qualified appraisal (Notice 2018:33 Effective January 1,2019)
Qualified appraiser -(1) IRS Definition. For purposes of section 170(f)(11) and §1.170A-16(d)(1)(ii) and (e)(1)(ii), the term *qualified appraiser* means an individual with verifiable education and experience in valuing the type of property for which the appraisal is performed, as described in paragraphs (b) (2) through (4) of this section.

(2) *Education and experience in valuing the type of property- (i) In general.* An individual is treated as having education and experience in valuing the type of property within the meaning of paragraph (h)(1) of this section if, as of the date the individual signs the appraisal, the individual has—

(A) **Successfully completed** (for example, received a passing grade on a final examination) *professional or college-level coursework*, as described in paragraph (b)(2)(ii) of this section, in valuing the type of property, as described in paragraph (b)(3) of this section, and has two or more years of experience in valuing the type of property, as described in paragraph (b)(3) of this section; or

(B) *Earned a recognized appraiser designation*, as described in paragraph (b)(2)(iii) of this section, for the type of property, as described in paragraph (b) (3) of this section.

(ii) *Coursework must be obtained from an educational organization, generally recognized professional trade or appraiser organization, or employer educational program.* For purposes of paragraph (b)(2)(i)(A) of this section, the coursework must be obtained from—

(A) *A professional or college-level educational organization* described in section 170(b)(1)(A)(ii);

(B) A generally recognized professional trade or appraiser organization that regularly offers educational programs in valuing the type of property; or

(C) An employer as part of an employee apprenticeship or educational program substantially similar to the educational programs described in paragraphs (b)(2) (ii)(A) and (B) of this section.

(iii) *Recognized appraiser designation defined.* A *recognized appraiser designation* means a designation awarded by a generally recognized professional appraiser organization on the basis of demonstrated competency.

(3) *Type of property defined—(i) In general.* The type of property means the category of property customary in the appraisal field for an appraiser to value.

(ii) *Examples.* The following examples illustrate the rule of paragraphs (b)(2)(i) and (b)(3)(i) of this section:

Example (1). Coursework in valuing type of property. There are very few professional-level courses offered in widget appraising, and it is customary in the appraisal field for personal property appraisers to appraise widgets.

Appraiser *A* has successfully completed professional-level coursework in valuing personal property generally but has completed no coursework in valuing widgets. The coursework completed by appraiser *A* is for the type of property under paragraphs (b)(2)(i) and (b)(3)(i) of this section.

Example (2). Experience in valuing type of property. It is customary for professional antique appraisers to appraise antique widgets. Appraiser *B* has two years of experience in valuing antiques generally and is asked to appraise an antique widget. Appraiser *B* has obtained experience in valuing the type of property under paragraphs (b)(2)(i) and (b)(3)(i) of this section.

Example (3). No experience in valuing type of property. It is not customary for professional antique appraisers to appraise new widgets. Appraiser *C* has experience in appraising antiques generally but no experience in appraising new widgets. Appraiser *C* is asked to appraise a new widget. Appraiser *C* does not have experience in valuing the type of property under paragraphs (b) (2)(i) and (b) (3)(i) of this section.

(4) *Verifiable.* For purposes of paragraph (b)(l) of this section, education and experience in valuing the type of property are verifiable if the appraiser specifies in the appraisal the appraiser's education and experience in valuing the type of property, as described in paragraphs (b)(2) and (3) of this section, and the appraiser makes a declaration in the appraisal that, because of the appraiser's education and experience, the appraiser is qualified to make appraisals of the type of property being valued.

For real property, the appraiser must be licensed or certified for the type of property being appraised in the state in which the property is located.

In addition, the appraiser must complete IRS Form 8283, section B, part Ill. More than one appraiser may appraise the property, provided that each complies with the requirements, including signing the qualified appraisal and IRS Form 8283, section B, part Ill.

Glossary of Terms

arm's length: a transaction in which the parties involved act independently of each other.

bargain sale: also called a donative sale or partial gift/partial purchase, a bargain sale of property (a sale or exchange for less than the property's fair market value) to a qualified organization is partly a charitable contribution and partly a sale or exchange.

bundle of rights: the concept that compares property ownership to a bundle of sticks with each stick representing a distinct and seperate right of the property owner, e.g., the right to use, to sell it, to lease it, to give it away, or to choose to exercise all or none of these rights (*Black's Law Dictionary*).

capital gain property: when individuals sell or dispose of property and realize an amount over the adjusted basis of that property, they have gain. Capital gains are gains from the sale or exchange of capital assets.

collections management policy: institutional policy document that establishes an institution's guidelines and standards for collections stewardship; covers responsibilities for recommending and implementing policy with respect to acquisition, collection growth, and deaccessioning; planning and establishing collection priorities; obtaining, allocating, and managing resources; and coordinating collection processes with the needs of the institution. "A collections management policy explains why a museum is in operation and how it goes about its business" (Marie C. Malaro, *A Legal Primer for Managing Museum Collections*, 2nd ed. Washington, DC: Smithsonian Institution Press, 1998).

cost basis: the original price of an asset, such as stocks, bonds, mutual funds, property, or equipment. Cost basis includes the purchase price and any associated purchase costs.

cultural patrimony: an object having ongoing historical, traditional, or cultural importance central to a group or culture itself, rather than property owned by an individual, and which, therefore, cannot be alienated, appropriated, or conveyed by any individual.

deaccession: the process used to permanently remove an object from a museum, library, or art gallery collection. Deaccessioning should result from a thoughtful, well-documented process, guided by established institutional collections management policy. The AAM Code of Ethics for Museums requires that funds from a deaccession be used only for acquisition or for direct care of the museum's collection and never for general operating expenses.

deed of gift: a written instrument or contract that transfers ownership of an object or objects from a donor to an institution; a legal museum document that conveys a gift and transfers title from a donor to a museum with an official date of the gift. This document should include all conditions of the gift. It must be signed by the donor and contain a signature of acknowledgment of receipt of gift by the institution.

disposal: the action taken after a deaccession decision. The institution's collections management policy should define appropriate methods of disposal of deaccessioned objects (e.g., transfer to a teaching collection, sale at public auction, donation to another institution).

donative sale. See *bargain sale.*

fair market value: the price that the property would sell for on the open market. It is the price that would be agreed on between a willing buyer and a willing seller, with neither being required to act, and both having reasonable knowledge of the relevant facts. (See section 1.170A-l(c) (2) of the Federal Income Tax Regulations and also Revenue Procedure 66-49, 1966-2 C.B. 1257.)

501 (C) (3) corporation: a nonprofit corporation formed to carry out charitable, educational, religious, literary, or scientific purposes. Federal and state governments do not generally tax nonprofit corporations on money they make that is related to their nonprofit purpose because of the benefits they contribute to society.

fractional gift: a donation of an object or collection of objects to which the museum does not receive full title immediately. A fractional interest gift is one in which the museum is given an initial fractional interest and the donor retains the remaining fractional interest. Under current tax law, a donor must complete the gift within 10 years or upon his or her death, whichever comes first. Also, the museum must take substantial physical possession of the gift over the course of the period of gift.

inter vivos gift: the transfer of property by agreement between living persons and not by a gift through a will.

IRS Form 8282: a form that must be filed by the donee organization if a donor of charitable property valued at more than $500 files Form 8283 and the donee organization sells, exchanges, or disposes of the donated property within three years. The donee organization must supply a copy to the donor. Also called a Donee Information Return form.

IRS Form 8283: a form for noncash donations. A donor must attach this form to his or her tax return to support a charitable deduction. It requires the date of gift and the signature of the donor, the accepting institution, and the appraiser. The donee organization must indicate if the gift was accepted for an unrelated use. This form must be filed if the value of all noncash contributions is more than $500. Section B must be completed for donations of over $5,000.

IRS Notice 2006-96: defines "qualified appraisal" and "qualified appraiser" for purposes of substantiating property for which a charitable contribution deduction in excess of $5,000 is claimed and for penalties for appraisals that result in substantial or gross valuation misstatement.

IRS Publication 526: explains how to claim deductions for charitable contributions. Discusses organizations that are qualified to receive deductible charitable contributions, the types of contributions that can be deducted, how much can be deducted, what records to keep, and how to report charitable contributions.

IRS Publication 561: a publication designed to help donors and appraisers determine the fair market value of property (other than cash) that is given to qualified organizations. It also explains what kind of object identification information is needed to support charitable contribution deductions as well as the required qualifications of an appraiser to meet IRS standards.

partial gift/partial purchase. See *bargain sale*.

related/unrelated gifts: with tangible personal property (TPP), the charitable deduction for a gift will depend on a categorization of the property as a "related" or "unrelated" use asset. A related use gift occurs when the charity actually makes use of the property in a manner consistent with its exempt purpose. However, a gift of tangible personal property for an unrelated use produces a deduction only for the lesser of cost basis or fair market value.

unencumbered title: title to real or personal property, free of liens or judgments, giving the named title holder legal rights of ownership.

Resources and Bibliography

American Alliance of Museums: www.aam-us.org

Internal Revenue Service: www.irs.gov

IRS Form 8282: www.irs.gov/pub/irs-pdf/f8282.pdf

IRS Form 8283: www.irs.gov/pub/irs-pdf/f8283.pdf

IRS Publication 526: www.irs.gov/pub/irs-pdf/p526.pdf

IRS Publication 561: www.irs.gov/pub/irs-pdf/p561.pdf

Buck, Rebecca, and Jean A. Gilmore, eds. *Museum Registration Methods*, 5th ed. Washington, DC: AAM Press, 2010.

Garner, Bryan A. *Black's Law Dictionary*, 11th ed. Toronto: Thomson Reuters, 2019.

Malaro, Marie C., and Ildiko Pogany DeAngelis. *A Legal Primer on Managing Museum Collections*, 3rd ed. Washington, DC: Smithsonian Institution Press, 2012.

Merritt, Elizabeth, ed. *National Standards & Best Practices for U.S. Museums*. Washington, DC: AAM Press, 2008.

Phelan, Marilyn E. *Museum Law: A Guide for Officers, Directors and Counsel*, 2nd ed. Lubbock, TX: Kalos Kapp Press, Texas Tech University, 2001.

Simmons, John E. and Toni M. Kiser, eds. *Museum Registartion Methods*, 6th ed. Lanham, MD: Rowman & Littlefield and the American Alliance of Museums, 2020.

Steiner, Christine, ed. *A Museum Guide to Copyright and Trademark*. Washington, DC: AAM Press, 1999.

Yeide, Nancy H., Konstantin Akinsha, and Amy L. Walsh. *The AAM Guide to Provenance Research*. Washington, DC: American Association of Museums, 2001.

Index

About the Editor and Contributors

Helen A. Harrison, the Eugene V. and Clare E. Thaw Director of the Pollock-Krasner House and Study Center in East Hampton, New York, is a former art reviewer and feature writer for *The New York Times* and visual arts commentator for National Public Radio. As the curator of the Parrish Art Museum and Guild Hall Museum on eastern Long Island, and guest curator at the Queens Museum in Flushing, New York, she organized numerous exhibitions prior to becoming the Pollock-Krasner House director in 1990. Among her many publications are exhibition catalogs, essays, reviews and articles, and several books, including monographs on Larry Rivers and Jackson Pollock; *Hamptons Bohemia: Two Centuries of Artists and Writers on the Beach*, co-authored with Constance Ayers Denne; and two mystery novels, *An Exquisite Corpse* and *An Accidental Corpse*, set in the art world.

MacKenzie L. Mallon is the provenance specialist at the Nelson-Atkins Museum of Art, Kansas City, Missouri, where she oversees provenance research, procedures, documentation, and review in conjunction with the curatorial departments. Mallon received her BA in history and MA in art history from the University of Missouri-Columbia. Her primary research interest is Nazi-era provenance and the art market during World War II. Mallon was the curator of record for the installation *Braving Shells for Art: The Monuments Men of the Nelson-Atkins* and is the author of *A Refuge from War: The Nelson-Atkins Museum of Art and the Evacuation of Art to the Midwest during World War II* (*Getty Research Journal*, February 2016). In addition to her work on provenance research and documentation, Mallon is currently studying the initial development of the Nelson-Atkins Museum collection during the early 1930s.

Laurette E. McCarthy, PhD, is an art historian and curator who specializes in American art and its confluences with multiple modernisms in the early 20th century. She received her BA from Tufts University, MA from the George Washington University, and PhD from the University of Delaware. She worked at The Phillips Collection and the National Gallery of Art and served as the George Gurney Senior Fellow at the Smithsonian American Art Museum in 2016–2017. She is the authority on American artist and critic Walter Pach, publishing *Walter Pach (1883–1958): The Armory Show and the Untold Story of Modern Art in American* in 2011.

She is also the foremost expert on the 1913 Armory Show. She has published numerous essays, curated/cocurated over a dozen exhibitions, lectured extensively, and appeared in two documentary art films. She was an accredited member of the American Society of Appraisers and chaired sessions on the IRS and Gifts and Donations to Museums at the American Alliance of Museums' 2008 and 2009 annual conferences. She was the chief compiler of IRS materials for the first edition of *To Give and To Receive* and served as coeditor of that edition as well.

Amy McKune is curator of collections at The National Museum of Toys and Miniatures, Kansas City, Missouri. Over the last thirty years, she has served as the director of museum collections at the Eiteljorg Museum of American Indians and Western Art (Indianapolis, Indiana), registrar/collections manager at the Museum of the Rockies (Bozeman, Montana), curator/collections manager at the Washington State Historical Society (Tacoma, Washington), and history curator at The Museums at Stony Brook (now The Long Island Museum, Stony Brook, New York). McKune earned her AB in anthropology from Kenyon College and her MA in history museum studies from the Cooperstown Graduate Program, SUNY-Oneonta. McKune has taught collections care and management as an adjunct faculty member for the University of Missouri–Kansas City, Indiana University Purdue University at Indianapolis, and Montana State University, Bozeman, Montana. She was a contributing author of *To Give* *and To Receive: A Handbook of Gifts and Donations for Museums and Donors* (AAM, 2011).

Beth J. Parker Miller serves as registrar for Winterthur Museum, Garden and Library (Winterthur, Delaware) and has more than thirty years' experience in museum collections management. Before joining Winterthur, she served as associate curator and registrar at Hancock Shaker Village (Pittsfield, Massachusetts) and as registrar at Hagley Museum and Library (Wilmington, Delaware). Parker Miller holds a BA in English and German and an MA in history with a concentration in archival and historical administration. Miller is a contributing author to *Museum Registration Methods*, 6th ed. (AAM, 2019), *The Shakers of White Water, Ohio, 1823–1916* (Richard W. Couper Press, 2014), and *To Give and To Receive: A Handbook of Gifts and Donations for Museums and Donors* (AAM, 2011).

Elizabeth Morton, PhD, is associate professor of art history, department chair of art, and curator of the Eric Dean and Greg Huebner Art Galleries at Wabash College. Her publications and research focus primarily on modern art workshops in Africa and American collectors of African art. Morton has many years of curatorial experience, including dozens of exhibitions at the National Museum and Art Gallery in Botswana, where she worked for four years through the Swedish International Development Authority. Most recently, she curated the reinstallation of African art at the Snite Museum of the University of Notre Dame and authored the catalog *Dimensions of Power* (South Bend: Snite Museum of Art, University of Notre Dame, 2018). Morton's curatorial projects also include the 2012 reinstallation of the Eiteljorg Suite of African and Oceanic Art and *Dynasty and Divinity: Ife Art in Ancient Nigeria* (2011–2012) at the Indianapolis Museum of Art at Newfields.

Luke Nikas and **Maaren A. Shah** are partners and co-chairs of the Art Litigation and Disputes practice in the international law firm of Quinn Emanuel Urquhart & Sullivan, LLP.

Luke Nikas is a leading commercial litigator with extensive experience representing clients in complex disputes, from trial through appeal. He led the defense in a forgery case dubbed by Art News as "The Art Trial of the Century," was named a 2019 Law360 MVP in media and entertainment litigation, and has been named to Lawdragon's List of the 500 Leading Lawyers in America. Among several other matters, he has recovered priceless works of art by Andy Warhol and Pablo Picasso; prosecuted and defended fraud, contract, negligence, and racketeering cases involving allegations of forgery and problematic provenance; located stolen artwork in foreign jurusdictions and countries; litigated disputes regarding art contracts and transactions, ownership of art, and transfers under the UCC; advised catalogues raisonné about litigation risk management; and handled numerous copyright and trademark matters for artists, companies, and foundations. He graduated magna cum laude from Harvad Law School.

Jeffrey H. Patchen, DME, serves as President and CEO of The Children's Museum of Indianapolis, former Senior Program Officer for National Programs at The J. Paul Getty Trust, Endowed Chair of Excellence in Arts Education at the University of Tennessee at Chattanooga, and State Music and Arts Consultant for the Indiana Department of Education.

Maaren A. Shah graduated with distinction from Stanford Law School and clerked for the Honorable Robert D. Sack on the Second Circuit U.S. Court of Appeals. She has extensive experience handling complex commercial disputes, including complex litigation, arbitration, and appeals. Shah has an art litigation practice representing clients in art-related disputes involving issues such as copyright/fair use, provenance and authenticity, art forgery, and art financing, and has handled matters relating to several contemporary artists, including Andy Warhol and Robert Indiana.

Robert B. Simon, PhD, President of Robert Simon Fine Art, New York City and Tuxedo Park, New York. Robert B. Simon is an art historian and art dealer in New York, specializing in Renaissance and Baroque paintings. He received his doctorate at Columbia University and has published and lectured widely on both art historical matters and on broader concerns relating to the authenticity, valuation, conservation, and commercial trade of works of art. Significant paintings, drawings, and sculptures from his gallery are to be found in major American museums, as well as in private collections worldwide. He is co-author of *Leonardo's "Salvator Mundi" & The Collecting of Leonardo in the Stuart Courts* (2019).

Christine Steiner specializes in art law, handling transactions on behalf of diverse art-realted clients such as collectors, artists, artists estates, foundations, museums, cultural organizations, auction houses, creative businesses, and universities. She has served as Secretary and General Counsel of the J. Paul Getty Trust, as Assistant General Counsel of the Smithsonian Institution, as Assistant Attorney General of Maryland for state colleges and universities, and as Principal Counsel of the Maryland State public education system.

Steiner is also an adjunct professor of law at Loyola Law School in visual arts law, and has been a visiting professor in programs of international art law in Florence, Italy and Cambridge, England. She speaks frequently on art law topics, currently serves on the editorial board of the *Journal of the Copyright Society of the United States*, and is active in the arts nationally. She has been recognized consistently by Best Lawyers, the prestigious national peer-ranking organization, for her contributions to Art Law.

Sharon Smith Theobald, ASA, editor, as the director of Art Museum of Greater Lafayette, has served as curator for over 100 exhibitions while developing The Baber Contemporary Painting and Sculpture Collection and the Fry/Pritsker Ceramic and Art Glass Collection and also led Purdue University's Krannert School of Management's Corporate Art Exhibition Program. She received her MS from Hofstra University, New York; completed graduate courses in art history at the New School in New York City and PhD studies at Purdue University; and has served on the faculty of The State University of New York at Stonybrook and Wilfrid University, Ontario, Canada. Theobald also served the American Alliance of Museums on the Accreditation Commission and as chair of the AAM Standing Professional Committee for Small Museum Administrators while chairing AAM Annual Meetings' Museum Sessions in New

York, Philadelphia, Boston, Chicago, and Indianapolis. She studied museum management with the British Council and museum directors from twenty-two countries in London, England. In 1992, Theobald launched Appraisal Associates International and has worked with corporate, museum, and university art collections while serving as an appraiser and adviser to both museums and donors. She was the coeditor of the *American Society of Appraisers' (ASA) Personal Property Journal* while teaching ASA appraisal writing courses at George Washington and Northwestern University, Rhode Island School of Design, and University of Missouri. Theobald was a contributing coeditor of *To Give and To Receive :A Handbook of Gifts and Donations for Museums and Donors* (AAM, 2011).

Romy M. Vreeland was the manager supervising acquisitions at The Metropolitan Museum of Art from 2001 through 2016. She was responsible for coordinating and reporting actions that affect title to works of art in the museum's collection and served as a point person for collections management policy information. She holds an MA in art history and museum studies from the University of Southern California and a BFA in art history from Syracuse University. She has been a member of American Alliance of Museums (AAM) and its Registrar's Committee and has presented at AAM annual meetings.